WELL VERSED

Go to www.WellVersedBook.com to find:

- Links to videos done by Dr. Jim Garlow for all 31 chapters
- Info regarding the audio version of *Well Versed*
- Study questions for all 31 chapters for small group discussions
- Help for small group leaders when leading a *Well Versed* discussion
- Scriptures printed out that are cited in each chapter
- Links to interviews Dr. Garlow has done regarding *Well Versed*
- An intriguing "Photo Gallery"
- The "editor's cuts," that is, sections deleted from *Well Versed* due to space limitations

WELL VERSED

BIBLICAL ANSWERS TO TODAY'S TOUGH ISSUES

JAMES L. GARLOW

ASSISTED BY AUDREA TAYLOR, FRANK KACER, AND GARY CASS

SALEMBOOKS
an imprint of Regnery Publishing

Salem Books™ is a trademark of Salem Communications Holding Corporation; Regnery® is a registered trademark of Salem Communications Holding Corporation

Cataloging-in-Publication data on file with the Library of Congress

ISBN 978-1-62157-550-4

Published in the United States by
Salem Books
An imprint of Regnery Publishing
A Division of Salem Media Group
300 New Jersey Ave NW
Washington, DC 20001
www.Regnery.com

Manufactured in the United States of America

10 9

Books are available in quantity for promotional or premium use. For information on discounts and terms, please visit our website: www.Regnery.com

CONTENTS

PART IV: ECONOMICS

PART V: LAW AND SOCIETY

I lovingly dedicate this book

To my wife Rosemary
who blesses me everyday in everyway.

And to
Janie
Jeremy
Riley
Aidan
Levi
Joshua
Lacy
Lukas
Jackson
Tyson
Jacob
Josie
James
Marlena
Patrick
Hailey
Zachary
Jazzlynn
Karl
Vanessa
Rebeka

INTRODUCTION

I grew up on a Midwestern farm with strong Christian parents and a close family. I went through a long academic journey including three master's degrees and a doctorate. I married while in graduate school. My wife and I adopted four children. My wife of forty-two years died of cancer. I later remarried, and combined, we have eight children and nine grandchildren; I love and am close with every one of them. This is the lens through which I view my life.

I am a follower of Christ, a pastor, a lover of the Church and the Word of God. I am shaped by all of these things. I am not an economist, though some of this book deals with the economy. I am not an attorney, though some of this book deals with law. I am not a judge, though some of this book deals with judicial issues. I am not a foreign affairs specialist, though some of this book deals with international issues. I am not a medical doctor, though some of this book deals with medical issues. I am in neither the military nor law enforcement, though some of this book deals with our nation's safety at home and abroad. I am not a social worker, though some of this book deals with community and social issues. I am not a reporter, though some of this book deals with journalism. I am not currently an educator, though I was formerly a university professor. But I *am* a student of *the Book*, the Bible, which is God's Word. God knows everything. I don't. Because He knows it all, my desire is to carefully unpack what He says about these and other topics.

I care deeply for people, both those who agree with me and those who do not. We live in a broken world, but does it have to be *this* broken? I am heartbroken to see so much human suffering. I believe that following the Word of God in governmental arenas would allevi- ate much human tragedy.

I recognize that understanding and interpreting the Bible can be challenging at times. I am a Protestant. I am an evangelical, although it appears the word *evangelical* has largely lost its meaning. I am the type of evangelical who believes that the Bible is totally authoritative. I believe that the Bible speaks not merely to personal, family, and church issues, but also to national, community, and governmental issues, *if we would take the time to listen.*

I also grasp that there are significant differences between the theocracy of ancient Israel of the Old Testament and the constitutional Republic in contemporary America. Furthermore, I grasp that there are significant differences between the early Church in the New Tes- tament operating in a Jewish nation controlled by occupying Roman military forces directed by an emperor and the constitutional Repub- lic in contemporary America.

Are there governmental principles from the Old Testament and New Testament that might apply to America today? I believe there are. I contend that when these are followed, much of human pain and misery can be reduced.

I do not believe that the real separation in America is Right versus Left, but rather *right* versus *wrong*. Some principles are right. Some are not. The ones found in the Bible are always right. When followed, they bring great blessings.

My calling is not ultimately to save a nation, America nor any other nation. My calling is to "love the Lord your God with all your heart and with all your soul and with all your strength and with all your mind" and "love your neighbor as yourself" (Luke 10:27). Yet part of loving my God and loving my neighbor is to attempt to connect the dots between how things are and how things could be *if we would embrace scriptural principles*. It is an act of love to my neighbor to make known what blessings could be ours *if we would understand government from the One who thought of government, and who even spoke of it as something that would be shouldered by His Son* (Isaiah 9:6).

Some of what I write will be obvious. Some of it might be new to you. Some of it might be controversial, though controversy is not my goal. Some of it may seem simply impossible—even idyllic, utopian, or unrealistic—to carry out. That may be true. But that does not change the fact that the Bible has principles that could bring greater peace and tranquility to our nation, states, communities, places of work, schools, churches, and homes.

I am fallible, as we all are. This is my best effort, at *this* time. In the future, I may see clearer, understand truths better, and have more matured and seasoned insights than what are written here. If you were writing this book, you might write it differently. My friend Professor Rob Staples once said of his own writing, "It's my story. When you write yours, you can write it however you want." Each of us has his or her view of reality. This is mine.

PART I

WHAT SHALL I SAY?

CHAPTER ONE

WHY ARE WE QUIET?

*I have always said and always will say that the
studious perusal of the Sacred Volume [the Bible]
will make us better citizens....*

—THOMAS JEFFERSON

P eople want to be taught more about the social and political issues of our day. In August 2015, respected pollster George Barna released the results of a survey that revealed this remarkable insight. But the survey also revealed an odd behavioral pattern. People who label themselves as *conservatives* do not speak up.

Why? The answer might surprise you. It is not because they are afraid. They are not fearful of being called derogatory names, such as *intolerant* or *hateful*. According to the survey, they are quiet for one reason: *they do not know what to say!* They do not know how to state a biblical basis for their convictions. This book was born while reading the results of that survey. The results revealed that theologically and politically conservative people hold deep convictions. They simply are not sure how to convey those beliefs.[1]

One year prior, a Pew Research poll revealed more quite surprising, and unanticipated, information: people want their churches and pastors to speak up on the social and political issues of the day.[2] You might not think that revelation particularly newsworthy, but it is. Only a few short years earlier, the overwhelming consensus was that they did *not* want pastors to speak out. But four years brought about a dramatic shift. The two responses switched places, with more people now saying they wanted pastors to *speak out*.[3] What caused this change? And what had caused pastors to be silent in the first place?

THE CHANGE POINT

Everything changed on July 2, 1954. Lyndon Baines Johnson returned from Texas after the election season of 1954 angry at two prominent businessmen—Frank Gannett (media) and H. L. Hunt (oil)—who had opposed him in his reelection bid for the Senate through their not-for-profit organizations. They had thought he was too soft on communism.[4]

When a bill overhauling the tax code was going through the Senate, Johnson added a few words to the proposal. What became known as the Johnson Amendment passed with no discussion and only a voice vote.[5] The amendment effectively silenced and muzzled all pastors. Here's why: nearly all churches are classified as not-for-profit 501(c)(3) charitable organizations by the IRS.

Johnson's amendment inadvertently made it illegal for a pastor, because of his affiliation with a not-for-profit organization, to endorse or oppose a candidate in a sermon. Johnson's legislative aide would later admit that they did not have churches and pastors in mind, only these two businessmen and their organizations.[6] You might think the unintended outcome to be a good thing. But consider the following facts. First, there are twenty-nine different 501(c) not-for-profit categories.[7] Only category 3, out of all of the twenty-nine categories, was suddenly silenced—the one that included America's churches!

Second, what it means to *oppose* or *endorse* a candidate is unclear. For example, if a pastor says, "Vote to oppose abortion," and one candidate is pro-life and the other one is pro-abortion, did the pastor endorse a candidate? The Internal Revenue Service (IRS) cannot give a clear answer to these questions.

Third, the First Amendment guarantees no governmental intrusion into the pulpit—at all. None. The IRS has no authority to be the pulpit police, dictating what any pastor can say from any pulpit. And they know it. At the urging of the Alliance Defending Freedom (ADF), a group of more than three thousand Christian and allied attorneys, several thousand pastors have intentionally violated the amendment since 2008 by endorsing or opposing a candidate from their pulpits. They then recorded their sermons and mailed them to the IRS.[8] Christian attorneys were prepared to defend these pastors. But the IRS has not taken a single church to court.[9] Why not?

The presumed answer is that the IRS does not want the Johnson Amendment to be scrutinized in the light of the U.S. Constitution, as it would most certainly be thrown out. However, for over sixty years, this unconstitutional law has been used to bludgeon, silence, censor, and muzzle pastors. I am not advocating that a pastor should or should not endorse or oppose a candidate. I am saying that it should be up to the pastor and that local church. The bottom line is that the First Amendment keeps the state from dictating what the church believes and practices.

Finally, a cultural myth has developed where people wrongly believe pastors *agreed* not to speak out on political issues in exchange for churches having tax-exempt status. Such is not the case. Our nation granted the tax-exempt status to churches from the beginning because the Supreme Court agreed that whatever the government could tax, it could kill. And if it could kill the church, there could be no true separation of church and state.

Many pastors have bought into the lie and gone silent. Pastors either don't know what to say regarding many social and political issues or won't say it. Many parishioners have become silent as well, and don't want their pastors to speak out. A silent pulpit means a silent pew. A silent pew produces an uninformed electorate. An uninformed electorate will not know what the One who created civil government has to say about how it should be run. To overcome this grand and lethal silence, this book was born.

THE BIBLE AND POLITICAL AND SOCIAL ISSUES

Does the Bible speak to the political and social issues of our day? To begin to answer that question, can we agree that our nation is in trouble?

There seems to be a strong consensus that our nation has problems—deep problems. No one thinks the massive debt is good.[10] Our national security has people on edge.[11] Waste, fraud, abuse, and corruption are widespread.[12] Civil discourse in governmental bodies is almost gone.[13] There is a strong sense among many that something has gone wrong.[14] For these reasons alone, continue to read the pages that follow, as they contain some good news regarding real answers that can make a difference.

The Bible speaks to every important issue of life. After all, it was God who came up with the idea of government. He established it and has clear principles about every major issue facing our nation or any nation. The Bible even uses the strong metaphor to say of Jesus: "The government will be on his shoulders" (Isaiah 9:6).

SEPARATION OF CHURCH AND STATE

Some of you are likely thinking, *But wait! Don't we have separation of church and state?* Where is that in the Constitution? It is not. Where is that in our national birth certificate, the Declaration of Independence? It is not. Then where does the phrase come from?

It comes from a letter written by Thomas Jefferson to the Danbury Baptists in Connecticut on January 1, 1802, in which he used the phrase "wall of separation" to assure them that the federal government would not intrude into church life (that is, forcing a certain denominational state church on the people).[15] But nowhere did he or any other Founder try to distance the federal government from the basic tenets of Christianity. On the contrary, the Bible was the book the Founders quoted most.

Many people like to point out that Jefferson was not a Christian, but a Deist. Yet he got on his horse Sunday after Sunday and rode down Pennsylvania Avenue from the White House to the Capitol Building for weekly interdenominational Christian worship services—complete with preaching by a pastor from the Bible.[16] In fact, there were weekly worship services in the U.S. Capitol Building from approximately 1800 to 1869.[17] The Founders affirmed this practice.[18] Weekly Christian worship services in our U.S. Capitol? So much for their believing in the present-day understanding of separation of church and state! After a 145-year hiatus, services were begun again on July 30, 2014, and are held every Wednesday night in the Capitol Building for members of Congress and their staff. These meetings are called the Jefferson Gathering in honor of the nation's third president.[19]

One more thing: How often do we hear someone say, *You can't legislate morality?* The fact is, all laws legislate morality. We have laws against murder because we believe that it is not right for people to murder. Laws against perjury (lying under oath), stealing, violating contracts—along with a host of other laws—are all attempts to legislate morality. Of course we legislate morality; that is the reason for laws.

THE WAY GOVERNMENT WAS INTENDED

Here is the good news: government—if properly ordered—*can* work. It *can* do what it is supposed to do. For just a moment, imagine with me that we could do away with the horrific messes we have in our national, state, and municipal governments right now. Suppose we could reconstruct government. What would it look like? What would make government function the way it is supposed to, bringing peace and tranquility to our communities?

That is exactly what we will uncover—or rather rediscover—in the pages that follow. As a result, I hope you will become *well versed* on more than thirty different political and social issues.

WHEN THE BIBLE SPEAKS, IMPLIES, OR STAYS SILENT

I readily acknowledge that the many issues we will cover are not equally weighted in Scripture. The Bible's response to the political and social issues of our day will fall into four categories:

- Cases where the Bible speaks directly and clearly to some issues. (An example would be the definition of marriage in Genesis and stated again by Jesus in Matthew.)
- Cases where the Bible speaks to overarching principles for today's issues. (An example might be the principles applied to minimum-wage laws.)

- Cases where there are biblical inferences regarding present-day social and political issues. (An example would be the biblical approach to appropriate taxation.)
- Those topics the Bible does not address via direct reference, overarching principle, or inference. (I choose not to discuss those topics.)

I write the following pages with a healthy sense of humility, recognizing that the truth of God's Word is more expansive than this author could possibly understand. With that in mind, let's move forward.

CHAPTER TWO

WHY SHOULD ANYONE LISTEN TO ME?

Do your best to present yourself to God as one approved,
a worker who does not need to be ashamed and who
correctly handles the word of truth.

—2 TIMOTHY 2:15, NIV

T he purpose of this book is to equip you to have biblical answers
to the tough issues of today, to make certain you are *well versed*
with verses and principles from Scripture. But you may ask yourself, *Why should anyone listen to me?* Fair question. In the following
pages, we will discuss the biblical approach and answers to many
vexing questions of our time. To the believer, this makes perfect sense,
because we are convinced of the truth and total reliability of the Bible.

While the Bible does not speak to every particular situation—and
that is important to acknowledge here—it does give us the necessary
moral framework and general principles to apply to every situation.
This includes guidance on how to understand today's most challenging

political and social issues and how to exercise our stewardship to vote. This book is designed to help you do just that.

"BUT THAT'S JUST *YOUR* INTERPRETATION OF THE BIBLE!"

My doctoral studies were in historical theology, or how beliefs develop throughout Church history. While it is true that some of the secondary or tertiary beliefs have modulated over the centuries, it is remarkable how the core biblical beliefs have remained largely intact for several thousand years across vastly differing cultural settings.

When you interpret what the Bible says, some people may say, *But that's just* your *interpretation of the Bible!* Not so. What is important is to (1) let the Bible speak for itself; (2) see how early followers of Christ understood it; and (3) follow how it has been understood through the centuries.

Hermeneutics is the science of interpretation. There are certain hermeneutical principles by which we make sense of what God is saying through the Bible. They are as follows:

1.   Holy Spirit: If you are a follower of Jesus, it makes sense to pray for the Holy Spirit to guide you. Allow me to suggest a prayer based on Ephesians 1:17–18: "(I ask) that… God…may give (us) the Spirit of wisdom and revelation, so that (we) may know him better. I pray also that the eyes of (our) heart(s) may be enlightened in order that (we) may know the hope to which he has called (us)…."
2.   Whole Bible: Allow the Bible to interpret itself. When a passage is not clear, allow the clear passages to be the interpreter.
3.   Literature: Know the type of literature you are reading, why the author wrote it, who it is written by and to whom, and the historical background.

4. Context: Understand context, the verses before and after.
5. Word study: What do the words mean? Understand idioms. For example, "when the sun went down" or "the four corners of the earth" are idioms. We don't actually believe the sun drops or the earth has corners.
6. Old Testament/New Testament connection: Understand that the Old Testament is moving toward the New Testament, and that the New Testament is founded upon, and makes no sense without, the Old Testament.
7. Literal: Take things literally unless the context tells you to interpret it figuratively. For example, where the verse says that God gathers us "like a mother hen gathers its chicks," it does not mean that God has feathers.
8. Revelation: What might God be revealing about Himself to humanity?
9. Principles: Carefully look for timeless principles. Distinguish between temporary commands (to the ancient Hebrew people) and permanent ones, which apply to us today. The Bible indicates that the prohibition against homosexual practice continues from the Old Testament into the New Testament. Yet some of the items listed there (mixing types of garments or mixing different kinds of seeds) applied specifically to a nomadic ancient people traveling among pagans.
10. Adherence: Avoid bending the text to say what you want it to say, reading something into the text that is not there. *Eisegesis* (pronounced "EYE-So-Gee-Sus") means putting one's view into a biblical text. *Exegesis* (pronounced "Ex-A-GEE-Sus") means finding meaning directly from the text. Beware of taking historical accounts and making them figurative. For example, just because Joshua marched around Jericho and the walls fell down is no reason for some young man to march around some woman seven

times hoping the walls of her heart will fall down. (I am
not making that one up!)

It is my goal throughout this book to approach the Bible with a
cautious awe, reverence, and respect, knowing it is possible to misuse
the text. Once again, some social and political topics have Bible verses
that speak overtly and clearly on the issues. Other issues are not referenced by name in the Bible, as in the case of abortion.[1] We can come
to a conclusion on other topics by biblical inferences. Thus, not everything covered in this book is biblically weighted the same.

JUDGE NOT

While we are talking about the use and abuse of Scripture, we
need to discuss the single most misused text in the Bible. In fact, I
am convinced that "Judge not" are the only two words some people
know in the entire Bible! Matthew 7:1–2 states, "Do not judge, or
you too will be judged. For in the same way you judge others, you
will be judged, and with the measure you use, it will be measured to
you."

It does *not* merely say, "Judge not!" It says, in effect, *Don't judge
someone else, unless you are willing to be judged by the same standard.* Mature, Bible-believing followers of Jesus are willing to be
judged by the same standard. Of course we are to judge! We all do. I
judge when I say that a man should not beat his wife. I judge when I
say that racial prejudice is sin. I judge when I say that a sex offender
should not molest little boys and girls. That is judging. And I am willing to be judged by the same standards.

Ironically, the people who are always proclaiming "judge not"
are themselves casting judgment. While telling others not to judge,
they have easily become trapped in this circular reasoning. Those
pushing the radical homosexual agenda and their coconspirators have

effectively marked out all of the Bible, including the clear and undeni-able prohibitions against the practice or act of homosexuality, except the words *Judge not*, presumably unaware of their inherent hypocrisy by using those two words.

We want to use—not abuse—the Bible, allowing it to say and mean exactly what it says and means.

"BUT THAT'S JUST YOUR *OPINION!*"

Not everyone shares my respect for the Bible. Perhaps you picked up this book unconvinced that the Bible is really all that valuable for contemporary issues. If that describes you, first, thank you for reading this, and second, please keep reading. For most unbelievers, the most common objection raised is that our reference to the Bible is simply a preferential appeal, and is merely one opin-ion among billions. Pronouncing our arguments to be arbitrary does not defeat them. Actually, it establishes our argument! How is that?

Without God, there are no unchanging moral laws and no logical processes for reasoning. One opinion is no better, more meaningful, or more logical than any other. Without God, life spontaneously formed from nothing by the unexplained power of matter plus time plus chance. The problem for the unbeliever is he or she—may I be blunt?—cannot live out his or her faith in a world ruled by chance. What do I mean by that?

If chance is the ultimate reality, our minds are necessarily mere accidents too. Our neurons, which seem to be logical, really fire ran-domly, giving us the illusion of a rational world and moral absolutes. We rely on laws of science, math, logic, and communication to make sense of the world. Unbelievers can't account for any of these in a world created by blind, impersonal chance. All of these laws need something that established order in the first place.

For example, gravity acts on everyone, even if they deny the laws of science. We throw people in jail if they don't abide by the rules of accounting and randomly bounce checks, because numbers and math actually mean something. The world is predictable—not random and chaotic—because God created the world and sustains it. It reflects His own reasonable nature. We expect gravity to work tomorrow and not arbitrarily stop, because of our view of God and His loving, superintending providence. Only predictability makes science possible. If matter changed chaotically, then any experiment we do today has no bearing on how things will act tomorrow.

Correspondingly, Christians believe words and math and science actually mean something and will not suddenly be meaningless tomorrow, because they reflect the mind of God, who does not change.

MAKING YOUR CASE WITH THE UNBELIEVER

So when an unbeliever says, "That's just *your opinion*," thank them for supporting your point. When they ask what you mean, point out their objection actually proves a creator exists. When they ask how, respond, *Do you believe your objection is logical and reasonable?* Of course, they will say yes.

Then ask them, *Where do logic and reason come from if the universe is merely the random accident of impersonal matter plus time and chance? If matter is all there is, why do we still place so much trust in logic and reason?*

For fun, pose to them that if the mind is merely random, chemical-electrical impulses, then how can you trust your own unbelieving thoughts? Unless you start with faith in the true and living God, you are reduced to inconsistency and foolishness.

REACTIONS TO YOU

In discussions such as this, one of two things will happen. Some might ignore you, because the real issue is not an intellectual one, but a moral or behavioral one. In other words, the issues are often not intellectual, but about not wanting to conform to God's ways in morals and ethics. Some, however, will be more open. They know they are spiritual rebels. Remember, the Word of God is self-evident truth. It does not need us to defend it; rather, we must proclaim it. Their own conscience agrees with the Word, because God writes His Law on their hearts.

It is to the Word and to their consciences that we ought to appeal. God's Word is "sharper than any two-edged sword" and will cut through unbelieving arguments. God did it with many of us—perhaps even with you—and by His grace and love, He will do it with them.

Yes, we believe the Bible is the Word of God and *the* standard of faith and life. If this is not true, then all we have are the arbitrary whims and opinions of our own imagination or those imposed upon us. Life is reduced to the adage "might makes right." This is the cruel and vicious Darwinian ethic of survival of the fittest. And that is why we must be *well versed.*

✦

CHAPTER THREE

WHAT IS NEEDED NOW

The ultimate test of a moral society is the kind of world that it leaves to its children.

—DIETRICH BONHOEFFER

et me give you a Bible quiz. How many of the following biblical characters do you recognize? Shammua, Shaphat, Igal, Palti, Gaddiel, Gaddi, Ammiel, Sethur, Nahb, Guel. Did you recognize any of those ten names? I doubt you recognized a single one of them. And, yes, they're all in the Bible. Why do you not remember hearing them? The short answer is *because they were wimps.* Nobody needs to remember their names. They were the ten spies in Numbers 13:4–5, 7, 9–15 who were cowards.

We do, however, remember the other two spies: Joshua and Caleb. Why? Because they were courageous, bold, and ready to charge forward. Nobody wants to run with wimps. Everybody likes winners. Wimps don't turn around nations that are in trouble. You and I can't afford to act like any of those ten unknown characters. It's time for us to be Joshuas and Calebs. It's time for us to have courage.

THE TROUBLING QUESTION

In our nation, we have:

- Churches with attendance as high as seventy thousand;
- Christian universities that, when you include their online enrollment, have over one hundred thousand students;
- Christian publishers selling millions and millions of dollars of books; and
- Christian radio and television networks that span the entire globe.

We have never seen such strong numbers for the Christian community. Yet our nation is, both figuratively and literally, going to hell. How on earth could that be possible?

Some pastors have the audacity to hide behind the following claim: *I just preach Jesus. I don't get involved in politics.* That sounds very noble. For the record, I also preach Jesus. For over one half-century I have preached Jesus and given invitations for people to receive Him as Savior and Lord.

Those who say they only preach Jesus mean that they are unwilling, ill-equipped, or perhaps even afraid to engage what the Scripture says about other issues. I truly believe it's important to preach Jesus. But it's also important to preach *what Jesus preached*, and that was the understanding of the Kingdom manifested on earth. That's why He taught the disciples to pray, "Thy Kingdom come. Thy will be done. On Earth as it is in Heaven."

What does it mean to preach the Kingdom? It simply means to preach about the authority of Jesus as expressed in the heart of believers which, in turn, impacts society and culture.

THE WESLEYAN EXAMPLE

I am part of a denomination called the Wesleyan Church. The Wesleyan Church was founded in 1843 when a group of Methodist pastors were informed they could not discuss the slave issue in the Methodist Church because it was—get this—too divisive.

In other words, alleged unity trumped biblical truth. The bold and well-versed pastors would not be silent, and thus were forced out of the Methodist Church at that time. They formed what was then called the Wesleyan Methodist Connection of America, now simply called the Wesleyan Church.

And they did not confine themselves to words alone. Some of the early Wesleyan church buildings were a day's journey apart so that its members could smuggle the slaves from the South to the North to freedom as a part of the Underground Railroad. This boldness made them many enemies. These men and their congregations endured prejudice, shootings, and even hanging attempts.[1] In fact, in one county in South Carolina, there was a saying: "There's not enough rope to hang all the Wesleyans."

Would my pastor friends who only preach Jesus have ignored the horrific suffering and mistreatment of slaves in the South in the pre–Civil War? I surely hope not. I hope they would have been bold and preached the fullness of the Word of God, including renouncing the systemic evil of slavery.

If the Civil War is too distant an example, let's focus on more contemporary issues. Would the pastors who say they only preach Jesus also have stayed silent during the civil rights movement in the mid-1900s? I surely hope not. I hope they would've spoken out regarding this injustice. Would the same pastors refuse today to speak out against the demonic, global plague of human trafficking? What about not speaking out regarding poverty, domestic abuse, or persecution?

When one well-known politically conservative leader told me recently that pastors should only preach Jesus, I asked him, "Are you suggesting that William Wilberforce, who gave so much fighting slavery, was wrong? Are you telling me that Dietrich Bonhoeffer, who laid down his life for truth during World War II in Germany, was out of place? Was Martin Luther King Jr. wrong for challenging the racism of his day?"

We all know that these great heroes of the faith were most certainly *not* wrong. They refused to narrow-cast their sermons or their teaching. They preached "the whole counsel of God."

PASTORS, CHURCHES, CHRISTIANS, AND THE POLITICAL

Some time ago I hosted a conference at our church called FUTURE Conference. We had fifty-six speakers. They spoke on the biblical understanding regarding racial healing, ministering to ex-offenders, prison reform, immigration, Israel, terrorism, healthcare, and about twenty other topics. Throughout the conference we had one concern: What are the *biblical* answers for these societal problems?

If the Bible really does have answers, then why are we as pastors afraid to speak out on these issues? The simple answer is that many pastors are afraid to be identified with a political party. As a rule of thumb, the majority of white evangelicals, who regard the Bible as totally authoritative, have tended to vote predominantly Republican. (The majority of the predominantly white liberal denominational pastors, who do not view the Bible as reliable, tend to vote Democratic. Many black pastors have tended to identify more closely with the Democratic Party.) Many white evangelical pastors are fearful of being over identified—or identified at all—with the GOP. Thus, in an attempt to remain neutral, they stay silent on critical social issues. This way they are protected from being labeled *political*.

Let me be clear. Our hope is *not* in a party. My friend Sammy Rodriguez says it best: "Our hope is not in the donkey or in the elephant, but in the Lamb." But that fact should not silence us from speaking out strongly—that is, biblically—on the issues, and working for competent candidates who deserve our support on *biblical* grounds.

Remember the four *P*s:

- First, know the (biblical) *principles*.
- Second, know the *policies* that flow from those principles.
- Third, based on sound principles and policies, come the *politics*, or political discourse, working out the legislative components.
- Fourth, ask who is the best possible *person*, or candidate.

As a side note, I frequently hear people object, "But I don't want to vote for the lesser of two evils." Well, until Jesus runs for office, all candidates are flawed, sin-impacted, less-than-perfect human beings. The fact is in *every* political race, you are, in effect, choosing from the lesser of two evils. That phrase is often an excuse not to be involved. We need to drop it from our conversation.

As an evangelical pastor, I am not in the hip pocket of any party, including the GOP. My hope does not abide in political parties. My hope is in God and His truths. I would work as a Republican, Democrat, or Independent based on one thing: *How can I be the greatest influence for Christ and help influence governmental integrity in our nation?*

NOT POLITICAL, BUT BIBLICAL: IMPLICATIONS FOR GOVERNMENT

But pastors are often afraid to speak out on biblical issues. Sometimes when a pastor *does* speak out on an issue—let's say, the definition of marriage—he or she might receive an e-mail on Monday morning saying, in effect, *Pastor, if you are going to be political then we may have to look for another church.* And their tithe checks will follow. Pastors, under great pressure for "nickels, noses, and numbers" often capitulate to those few persons who say, *Don't be political.*

Allow me to demonstrate the truncating of the biblical message:

- If a pastor would have said fifty years ago that tearing up a baby in the womb is a bad thing, people would have responded, *Of course it is.* Say it today, and some will say, *Pastor, you are being too political.*
- If a pastor would have said thirty years ago that the practice of homosexuality is regarded as an abomination to God, people would have agreed, *Of course it is.* Say it today, and some will say, *Pastor, you are being too political.*
- If a pastor would have said fifteen years ago that marriage is between one man and one woman, people would have said, *Of course it is.* Say it today, and some will say, *Pastor, you are being too political.*
- If a pastor would have said ten years ago that God still has plans for Israel, people would have said, *Of course He does.* Say it today, and some will say, *Pastor, you are being too political.*

- If a pastor would have said eight years ago that the national debt is too high and is immoral, people would have said, *Of course it is.* Say it today, and some will say, *Pastor, you are being too political.*
- If a pastor would have said five years ago that socialism is a bad thing, people would have said, *Of course it is.* Say it today, and some will say, *Pastor, you are being too political.*

You get the picture. Pastors are being painted into a corner. Perhaps they have allowed themselves to be boxed in. Instead of being censored by others—whether by alleged IRS threats, by left-wing organizations' threats, or by threats from their congregants, pastors have self-censored. When a prominent, highly visible pastor was featured a few years ago on *Larry King Live*, he could not quite bring himself to say, "Jesus is the only way to Heaven" (John 14:6).[2] He is not alone. Out of fear of offending, some pastors self-muzzle or self-censor.

Throughout this book, I am not calling for political activism, although political activism is a very good thing. Merely being politically active means supporting a candidate and maybe voting every two years. *I am calling for something so much more exhilarating, foundational, and transformational, and that is what I call* biblical applicationalism, *which is the actual practical understanding and application of scriptural solutions to today's most challenging social and political problems.*

CHRISTIANS IN THE CULTURE

Given the realities of our present cultural situation in America, how should we respond when biblical values are under attack?

In the April 5, 1999, issue of *Christianity Today*, an article about Billy Graham stated that the secret of his ministry was his capacity to "engage, yet transcend" culture.[3] That is fascinating.

Most of us do one or the other. Either we engage culture and capitulate to worldly values, or we transcend culture and have no meaningful conversation with people who are different than us. The secret is to engage, yet transcend, be relevant to the unbelieving culture around us, while not losing our distinctive biblical values.

This was a problem for ancient Israel. They were consistently compromising with the pagan cultures around them. And this is a problem for contemporary Christians. The secret is to connect with this world, but not embrace its values.

OPEN THE CONVERSATION

I have tried to maintain a conversation with those with whom I most disagree. I have—on more than one occasion—phoned persons most hostile to my values and asked, "Can I ask you a favor? Will you give me one hour of your time to coach me? Will you give me one hour of your time to teach me how to connect with you?" And I have never been turned down. They have come. We have met. We have both learned a lot. This exercise is not merely about forming friendships. It is about speaking truth, something that is in rather short supply in today's culture.

After a heated battle defending traditional marriage in California (Proposition 8), I invited two people who held exactly opposite views from mine to the stage of my church for an evening seminar on discourse. One of them was the national "poster child" for same-sex "marriage." In addition, I invited another person who is homosexual and had authored a book on the topic of same-sex "marriage."

I began the evening by explaining to the nearly packed house— our auditorium seats two thousand—that our views on traditional marriage had not changed. But we also longed to model and demonstrate civil, respectful, thoughtful discourse. And we achieved the goal.

Due to these dialogues, I have formed relationships with some fairly well-known persons whose values totally contradict mine. And I value these relationships. Some might be inclined to criticize my practice. But remember, if Jesus chose to form friendships with the unacceptable people of his time (Mark 2:16), should we do any less?

I want to challenge you to do what I do: reach out to those you feel are most hostile to your biblical values, those with the greatest influence, and ask them if they would meet with you to have a civil dialogue. Admittedly, some may not. But most will. And there is great value in it.

STANDING ALONE

Hodge Chapel, designed by the brilliant scholar Dr. Timothy George, is a breathtaking structure located at Beeson Divinity School, part of Samford University in Birmingham, Alabama. It has a rotunda similar to the U.S. Capitol Building.

Well-known figures from church history are painted all the way around the rotunda. In addition, a large wood carving of four famous persons forms the front of the massive pulpit. Niches are adorned with busts of famous figures. When I had the privilege to preach there, I changed my sermon to tell the stories of the figures who seemed to be looking down on us. Over my left shoulder, one prominent figure stared at the crowd, a bust towering above us all. Everyone recognized him, in part because of the conspicuous spectacles. It was Dietrich Bonhoeffer.

"Why is he up there?" I asked, pointing to him. "It was because he had the biggest church in Germany. Oh, no, that wasn't it." I paused. "He is up there because he had so many bestsellers. Oh, no, he didn't— not during his lifetime." Again I paused. "He is remembered in this grand chapel because he had the biggest radio and TV ministry during that time. Oh, no, he didn't." Now I waited longer. "So how did he get up there? Why is his bust here in this grand hall? Let me tell you why. It was because they took him out into cold German air on the morning of April 9, 1945, and hanged him—because he would not compromise his biblical values! That is how he got there. And it is time for you as pastors to stop telling the stories of Bonhoeffer and become willing to be like him!"

A few years before Bonhoeffer's execution, Adolf Hitler met with a group of pastors in Berlin telling them to take care of the church, but to leave the state to him. Where do we hear that kind of thinking today? Hitler said, "I will be your Fuhrer (leader)."[4]

One pastor, Martin Niemoller, said, "No, you are not my Fuhrer. God is my Fuhrer!"[5] At that moment, the other pastors in the room, we are told, both physically and ideologically moved away from him. Who do we remember years later? Niemoller. We don't know the others. They were wimps.

THIS IS YOUR MOMENT

An elderly former Marine and retired college math professor in my church shocked me one day with these words: "I was a good Marine, but I never got a chance to prove it."

"What do you mean, Dennis?" I asked. He replied, "I was a Marine after the Korean War but before the Vietnam War. Since I was between wars, I never got a chance to fight. I never got a chance to prove what a good Marine I was."

You were not born between wars. We are alive in a time of tumultuous ideas and concepts. We are in a war: a war for truth, righteousness, and justice. The pages that follow are designed to equip you for success in those battles.

Welcome to the war.

PART II

RELIGION IN THE PUBLIC SQUARE

CHAPTER FOUR

THE PURPOSE OF GOVERNMENT

Our Constitution was made only for a moral and religious people. It is wholly inadequate to the government of any other.

—JOHN ADAMS, SECOND PRESIDENT OF THE UNITED STATES

I hear it said frequently: *All politicians are liars. Throw the bums out—all of them!* I strongly disagree. As one who has known and knows many successful politicians, I can name so many who have served or are serving their communities, states, and nation nobly.

Politics is not a dirty word. In fact, it is a calling to be highly respected. The reason so many people have a negative view of politics is that the government is failing to be what a government is supposed to be. That raises the obvious and foundational question: *What is the purpose of government?*

The primary purpose of government is to protect its citizenry by restraining evildoers. The best and simplest outline of government was written two thousand years ago by a man named Paul in a letter to his friends in the city of Rome. He wrote: "Everyone must submit himself to the governing authorities, for there is no authority except that which God has established. The authorities that exist have been established by God" (Romans 13:1). Seven hundred years earlier, a preacher named Isaiah stated: "For the Lord is our judge, the Lord is our lawgiver, the Lord is our king; it is he who will save us" (Isaiah 33:22).

Some secularists get nervous when they hear God referenced in such a prominent way in political conversation. Frankly, if they have a problem with that, they need to take it up with our national Founders who—contrary to the wishful thinking of revisionist historians—borrowed heavily from the Bible and its themes. Even Benjamin Franklin thought that Moses and the parting of the Red Sea should be the Great Seal of the nation.[1]

These same secularists panic that we are advocating a theocracy, in which religious rulers would govern based on what God has spoken. Their fears are in vain, as we live not in a theocracy but in a constitutional (this document is the law of the land) republic (where representatives are elected to represent us). To affirm God's role in government is not to call for a theocracy; rather, it reaffirms our Founders' position that our rights come from God.

"BY THEIR CREATOR"

Government was established by God. Our national birth certificate, the Declaration of Independence, affirms that *all authority comes from God* when it states that all men are "endowed by their Creator" with rights—in fact *unalienable* rights, rights that cannot be taken away, because they were given by God!

President Barack Obama—for whatever reason—omitted the important words "by their Creator" in reference to our unalienable rights in two written proclamations (February 2, 2009,[2] and September

17, 2009[3]) and in at least two speeches (September 15, 2010,[4] and September 22, 2010[5]). Is that accidental? I cannot assign motives, but it should concern us all that these words have been left out with such frequency. Why? *Because if our rights come from God, they cannot be taken by government—or any other persons.*

Our goal is not to somehow produce a theocracy. Our goal is for our government to protect our *God-given* rights. Paul stated, "He who rebels against the authority is rebelling against what God has instituted, and those who do so will bring judgment on themselves" (Romans 13:2). He further stated that people who do right need not fear the government. However, those who do wrong should be in terror: "But if you do wrong, be afraid, for he does not bear the sword for nothing. He is God's servant, an agent of wrath to bring punishment on the wrongdoer" (Romans 13:4).

As if that was not clear enough, he continued, "Therefore, it is necessary to submit to the authorities, not only because of possible punishment, but also because of conscience" (Romans 13:5). One of Jesus' closest friends, Peter, said that the role of government was "to punish those who do wrong and to commend those who do right" (1 Peter 2:14).

EVIL EXISTS

To agree with these purposes of government, one has to agree that evil actually exists. If you are inclined—like some are—to say *no, it does not exist*, then consider the name Hitler. Consider ISIS with its fatwas, explicitly detailing how to rape female sex slaves[6] and kill women and children for refusing to fast during Ramadan.[7]

Evil also exists much closer to home—within you and me. The prophet Jeremiah said some 2,700 years ago, "The heart is deceitful above all things and beyond cure. Who can understand it?" (Jeremiah 17:9). Listen to the talking heads debating or arguing on Fox News

Channel, MSNBC, or CNN. Often the difference boils down to *the acknowledgement or the denial of the existence of evil.*

THE LINE IN THE SAND

There are basically three ways of viewing humanity, or a doctrine of humankind, if you will:

1. Humanity is basically good; thus any problems are caused by lack of funding or lack of education.
2. Humanity is basically evil; thus it needs to be controlled by dictators and tyrants. (Ironically, the controllers are equally evil.)
3. Humanity was originally made good, in the image of God, but sin entered the human race; thus humans have great capability for evil, but Jesus entered the world to take on Himself the sins for all who repent and the Holy Spirit empowers one to live in righteousness.

Radio personality Dennis Prager rightly calls the belief in the existence of evil the "line in the sand" in all political discourse. He stated, "No issue has a greater influence on determining your social and political views than whether you view human nature as basically good or not. In twenty years as a radio talk show host...I realized that perhaps the major reason for political and other disagreements I had with callers was that they believed people are basically good, and I did not."[8] Prager continues, "First, if you believe people are born good, you will attribute evil to forces outside the individual."[9]

Prager noted that some liberal politicians actually believe that the reason Islamists destroy others and themselves is because of exterior issues, such as poverty. In other words, they cannot believe that these people could possibly be evil. He closes with these foreboding words:

"If the West does not...begin to recognize evil, judge it, and confront it, it will find itself incapable of fighting" those who would destroy us.[10] Succinctly stated, evil exists. In all of us. And it has to be dealt with.

The restraining of evil includes trying to restrain evil *in government itself*. This is profoundly demonstrated by the fact that we have three branches of government: executive, legislative, and judicial. They have to keep each other in check because of the capacity for evil in the human heart—including those in political leadership. The fact that we have three supposedly equal branches of government is an acknowledgement by our Founders of a deeply held theological truth: humans are capable of evil.

Our Founding Fathers knew and understood evil. They had fled evil in their homelands. They attempted to construct a new government that would hold evil in check, even within government itself. That is why the Bill of Rights limits government. The failure to fully understand the capacity of evil within government was demonstrated by both President Franklin Roosevelt (January 11, 1944) and President Barack Obama when they both suggested—many decades apart—that there should be a Bill of Rights *for* the government.[11] Bluntly stated, the government doesn't need more rights. We need protection as citizens, often times *from* our government.

Remember the Bill of Rights are the rights for citizens and are designed to restrain government. But these two presidents wanted a Bill of Rights *for* the government. That view indicates an inadequate and unsophisticated understanding of the nature of evil and the damage that can be done by an unrestrained government.

CHAPTER FIVE

FIRST AMENDMENT AND RELIGIOUS LIBERTY

Congress shall make no law respecting an establishment of religion, or prohibiting the free exercise thereof; or abridging the freedom of speech, or of the press; or the right of the people peaceably to assemble, and to petition the government for a redress of grievances.

—FIRST AMENDMENT TO THE CONSTITUTION OF THE UNITED STATES OF AMERICA

It's called our First Freedom: the freedom to exercise our faith in accordance with the dictates of our own consciences. The Founders declared there would be no established U.S. national church like the model of European nations. The individual states would be free to exercise their respective Christian denomination, if they wished, and the federal government would not interfere.

This was a wonderful and unique American liberty rooted in the ideals of Christian tolerance. We must not bind the conscience of another person and force him to worship or hold religious views contrary to his own faith. Because the United States was for the most part a Christian nation with a common moral framework and common law, it worked well. Unfortunately, this right has been hijacked and distorted beyond recognition.

We must be very careful not to assume the right to do anything we want in the name of practicing our religion. There have always been limits on religion in America. If our rights are God given, they must be exercised under His terms. There is no right to start the First United Cannibal Church, for example. Warren Jeffs, former president of the Fundamentalist Church of Jesus Christ of Latter-Day Saints, is currently serving a sentence of life plus twenty years on two felony counts of child sexual assault.[1] Religious liberty is not a license for abuse.

THE LOSS OF RELIGIOUS LIBERTY

Unfortunately, Christian religious tolerance has devolved into a secular monstrosity called multiculturalism. This unbelieving system of thought rejects the Founders' views in exchange for religious relativism. According to this view, all religions are essentially the same, therefore they all must be treated equally.

All religions are not the same. Every religion has its own unique worldview and a corresponding system of ethics that produces its own culture. Simply travel to India and find the caste system based on the Hindu doctrine of reincarnation. Go to Saudi Arabia and find Muslim male superiority and no religious tolerance. Travel to communist China and see the elitist totalitarianism based on the religion of humanism.

All religions, including the religion of secular humanism, are based on some authority. America was founded on the "Laws of nature and Nature's God."[2] Everyone at that time knew this was a reference to the God of the Bible and His revealed laws in the Bible. Secularism is based on the idea that there is no God, and therefore only man can prescribe what is right. It always results in tyranny.

Islam subscribes to the Koran, the example of Muhammad, and his god Allah. Consequently, Islam perpetually wages its "holy war," called jihad, to conquer the world by any means necessary, including suicide bombing the women and children of non-Muslim infidels. The fact that the majority of the world's 1.6 billion Muslims are peaceful does not help those who have been killed or maimed by the 10 to 20 percent—a rather staggering number of persons—who use violence.

The heightened cultural tensions in America are a tug-of-war between competing religious ideologies of humanism, encroaching Islam, and our Judeo-Christian heritage. Now, more than ever, we need to embrace the spirit of the First Amendment and exercise our right to speak truth: the self-evident, biblical truth *on which the nation was founded.*

BASIC FREEDOMS

Freedom of religion and its corollary, freedom of speech, are paramount to a free people and government of, by, and for the people. It has been said you can know who is truly in power simply by discovering who it is unlawful to criticize.

For self-government to thrive, the people must have the right to confront government officials with political and moral grievances. Biblically speaking, we are tapping into the glorious prophetic tradition dating all the way back to Elijah. There are times when a John the Baptist must call out a Herod (Matthew 14:3–4) or a Nathan must expose a King David (2 Samuel 12). Of course, this is not without risk. It cost John the Baptist his head (Matthew 14:9–10). Stephen asked if there were any Old Testament prophets the Pharisees and their ancestors did not kill for their scathing spiritual and moral indictments (Acts 7:52).

We have the God-given right and duty to speak to and for God, and to live according to His will. We have the right and duty to speak to God in prayer and worship. No legitimate government can infringe on our private or corporate worship of the Lord—giver of our right to life, liberty, and the pursuit of virtue—or public expression of religion.

We also have a duty and a right to speak to other persons. The Lord Jesus Christ, the Creator, redeemer, and judge of all men, commands us to share the Gospel to all. No legitimate government can infringe on our declaring the only Truth that can save and redeem our fellow human beings. We are commanded to expose the unfruitful works of darkness. Out of love for our neighbor, we can't keep silent.

The Founders knew government is a leviathan that must be kept in check. So they divided, enumerated, and limited its powers. But, for the people of a society to remain free, they need free speech, a free press, and the ability to peacefully assemble to redress their grievances to safeguard their God-given rights.

Unbelieving persons might be offended by both Christ's Gospel and God's Law. Yet, we know that apart from the spectacular forgiveness of Jesus, a man's soul will be damned. Apart from God's Law, man will turn the earth into a tyrannical hellhole. We must face their attempts to silence us with boldness and grace.

THE FOCAL POINT

In much of present-day America, the battle to maintain the First Amendment has boiled down to the issues surrounding homosexual behavior. One could not have conceived of that fifty, or even twenty-five, years ago. *The coerced acceptance of homosexual behavior and the obvious counterpart of homosexual marriage has become the vortex for the crushing of the first portions of America's precious Bill of Rights.*

Modern hate-speech laws have been introduced in nations like England to great effect in shutting down the truth Christians are commanded to proclaim.[3] Thankfully, the First Amendment acts as a firewall to keep us free to proclaim the truth, but that has not kept the radical humanists from using our speech to persecute us.

For several years I recorded one-minute commentaries, aired on 850 radio outlets daily, covering lawsuits in which Christians were being defended by some of the three thousand allied attorneys of the Alliance Defending Freedom (ADF). In session after session, a similar pattern emerged: religious liberty be damned! The radical homosexual activists were determined not merely to be able to have their believed rights, but to coerce every unyielding person to accept and affirm their lifestyle actions. In case after case, deviant behavior overshadowed the First Amendment.

Christians are fired for holding politically incorrect positions.[4] Businesses are fined or closed because they refuse to support or celebrate sinful homosexual marriages.[5] Religious liberty is under attack from godless, sexual anarchists who believe they have a right to sexual antinomianism. There is no God-given *right* to do wrong. Every sinful act is by definition a lawless one.

The homosexual activists have been very successful propagandizing their movement by appealing to emotions; after all, *love is love*. In contrast, Scriptures tell us explicitly, "Love does not rejoice in wrongdoing, but rejoices in truth" (1 Corinthians 13:6, ESV). Regardless of contemporary culture's inability to grasp the truth in a hypersexualized setting, sex outside of the covenant of heterosexual marriage is always wrongdoing and is ultimately harmful to the person and society.

Lawless sexuality is not a victimless crime. Our children's bodies and souls will suffer from selfish, hedonistic sexuality. Women especially suffer the brunt of the consequences with out-of-wedlock pregnancies and births, coerced abortions, poverty, etc. Individuals and society pay dearly when we reject God's gracious and life-giving laws.

The good news is that time and eternity are on the side of Truth, as followers of Jesus are *well versed*, following their duty to proclaim and patiently explain truth. We have seen the consistent faithfulness of the Authentically Biblical Church ("ABC") turn the tide on the abortion issue, and we will win on God's honorable institution of marriage as well.

That's not to say it will be easy or without sacrifice and suffering. This is a time to have courage and do the work of the Kingdom of God in the power of the Spirit of the Living God. It is a remarkable thing to have the privilege of sharing Christ's power and to use our constitutionally guaranteed First Amendment rights to articulate a well-versed understanding of community and national life. The good news? Truth eventually wins. Be encouraged.

CHAPTER SIX

SCHOOLS, UNIVERSITIES, AND THE CHRISTIAN FAITH

*A Bible and a newspaper in every house, a good school
in every district—all studied and appreciated as they
merit—are the principal support of virtue, morality,
and civil liberty.*[1]

—BENJAMIN FRANKLIN

E ducation in America has come a long way from the one-room
schoolhouse model filled with children of all ages. I know. I grew
up in one. Each morning I rode my bicycle across Kansas State
Highway 9, up a steep incline, and across the Missouri Pacific Railroad tracks. I panted heavily as I pedaled up the hill, past my father's
pastures dotted with white-faced Hereford steers, past the country
cemetery where my grandparents and great-grandparents are buried,
and past the beautiful Magaw's Meadow, known for its great sledding
in winter. I was serenaded by the singing of Meadow Larks, the Kansas state bird. Finally, I steered to the left and arrived at District
Number 6, more affectionately known as Hillcrest School, a one-
room building with all eight grades (we had no kindergarten then). I

loved this little school, which prepared me well for high school, college, three master's degrees, and a doctorate.

But that Norman Rockwell America is gone today. Bibles once served as school readers in America. Faith was an integral part of a child's life inside the classroom. Today, almost every resemblance of Christianity has been banned from our state-funded schools.[2]

WHAT HAPPENED?

Certain roots of our current faithless educational system can be traced back to the prominent secularist, John Dewey. Dewey was a committed humanist who believed in using public schools to accomplish social reform and reconstruction, while rejecting the notion of divinely revealed truth or man being made in the image of God.[3] His influence on the direction and content of public education laid the foundation for educational legal battles that have emerged over the last generation.

One of those key judicial decisions came from the U.S. Supreme Court in 1962. In *Engel v. Vitale*, the court ruled that it was unconstitutional for state officials to compose an official school prayer and encourage its recitation in public schools. The inevitable consequence was a long process of removing any Christian influence from publically supported school environments and replacing it with politically correct philosophies. A sampling of these decisions includes the following:

- 1963: *Abington School District v. Schempp*—The U.S. Supreme Court ruled that school-sponsored Bible reading was unconstitutional.[4]
- 1980: *Stone v. Graham*—The Ten Commandments displayed in the classroom was ruled unconstitutional.[5]

- 1985: *Wallace v. Jaffree*—The court ruled a ban on the "moment of silence," which encouraged students to pray.[6]
- 1992: *Lee v. Weisman*— The court ruled prayer led by members of the clergy at public graduation ceremonies unlawful.[7]
- 2000: *Santa Fe Independent School Dist. v. Doe*— Student-led prayer was banned from high school football games.[8]

Not only are these (and many other) rulings hostile to expressions of Christian faith, but they've sent a chilling wind throughout the educational system to remove any vestige of religious belief, no matter how minor or individually practiced. Is this an overstatement?

The examples of anti-Christian bias throughout our nation now number in the tens of thousands. A first grader in Temecula, California, for example, had her Christmas presentation cut short for talking about her family's tradition centered on the Star of Bethlehem sitting atop her Christmas tree.[9] In the small town of Kountze, Texas, high school cheerleaders were sued for displaying Bible verses on their banners and posters.[10] A high school football coach was put on paid administrative leave after failing to comply with a school order to stop praying on the field with his players—and with whomever else wanted to join him—at the end of games in Bremerton, Washington.[11] In Los Angeles, a young boy suffering from cerebral palsy was barred from performing a Christian song at an after-school talent show until attorneys with Alliance Defending Freedom intervened.[12] Melville High School in New York prohibited students from simply forming a Christian club.[13] Clearly, one of the biggest spiritual wars in our culture is the battle in our schools for the very hearts and minds of our children.

TWENTY-FIRST-CENTURY EDUCATION RESULTS

Secularists have clearly misdiagnosed our education problems. They point to lack of funding and poor school standards with continually failing solutions, like Common Core (see chapter 9 for more information on Common Core). When we take a close look at Washington's attempt to fix education, we have to ask ourselves if the problem is really a lack of standards and funding, or if it is linked to something else.

Historian David Barton points out the correspondence between the removal of Christian influence in public school (beginning with *Engel v. Vitale*) and the obvious moral decay of our nation. Remove the moral anchor of Christian influence from one of the most powerful influencers of the next generation and we see the following happen in the years following 1963:

- Pregnancies in girls fifteen through nineteen years old increased 187 percent in the next fifteen years, and they increased 553 percent in girls aged ten through fourteen years old.
- Sexually transmitted diseases increased by over 226 percent in the next twelve years.
- Divorce rates increased over 300 percent each year for the next fifteen years.
- Single parent families rose by 140 percent.
- Unmarried couples living together increased by 353 percent.
- Violent crime increased by 544 percent.
- SAT scores declined for eighteen consecutive years following the removal of prayer from public schools, despite the fact that the same test from 1941 was being used.[14]

One would think that these statistics—and many others that could be provided—would cause secularists to enthusiastically embrace a biblically based, ethically and morally founded philosophy of education that infuses godly values with knowledge and skill development. Not so. Many naively believe that *there is no correlation between the removal of Christianity from public education and the horrific cultural realities.*

COLLEGES AND UNIVERSITIES

Christianity was not only removed from elementary and secondary education, but was also stripped from colleges and universities. A good handful of America's most prestigious universities were founded as Christian institutions. But look at them today, and you might never have guessed. Here are a few facts about Harvard University you may not know:

- Harvard University was founded because John Harvard willed some money and his library collection of 320 books to be used to educate young Christian men in ministry.[15]
- Harvard University's official school motto in 1692 read *Veritas christo et ecclesiae*—meaning *Truth for Christ and the Church.* Later, the last part was dropped off, and the motto on the school seal simply read *Veritas*— or *Truth.*[16]
- In Harvard's original *Rules and Precepts* of 1646 was this instruction: "Let every student be plainly instructed, and earnestly pressed to consider well, the main end of his life and studies is, to know God and Jesus Christ which is eternal life (John 17:3) and therefore to lay Christ in the bottom, as the only foundation of all sound knowledge and Learning. And seeing the Lord only giveth wisdom, Let every one seriously set

himself by prayer in secret to seek it of him (Proverbs 2:3)."[17]

Yale University's early motto included the Hebrew words *Urim* (lights) and *Thummim* (perfections) on its seal. The Hebrew school motto was clarified to mean, "Christ the Word and Interpreter of the Father, our light and perfection."[18] These are just two of numerous universities founded with strong Christian roots.

Nearly all of the Ivy League institutions were founded for the purpose of perpetuating the Gospel of Christ.[19] Many, if not most, of their early presidents were highly trained pastors.[20] But the Ivy League colleges' disengagement from their distinctly Christian roots forms one of many waves of loss of a moral and biblical center among colleges. And now, even most contemporary Christian colleges have unhitched from the Christian denominations that founded them. That may sound unimportant, until one tracks the consequential changes.

Further problems with so-called Christian academia came to light when three Mennonite schools—Bluffton University, Eastern Mennonite College, and Goshen College—decided to no longer follow Scripture, and hired employees involved in same-sex "unions."[21] This set off a reaction in the CCCU (the Coalition of Christian Colleges and Universities), an organization of approximately 180 Christian colleges around the world, including 117 in North America.[22] Three CCCU members' schools—Union College (Tennessee), Masters College (California), and Oklahoma Wesleyan University—seeing that CCCU would no longer stand for scriptural truth on the issue of homosexuality and marriage, left the organization.[23] The three Mennonite schools affirming homosexual behavior later withdrew from CCCU.[24] But the damage had been done and the true colors revealed. During the brouhaha, it was discovered that the vast majority of the Christian college presidents were comfortable with having colleges that affirm homosexual behavior as "affiliates" of a Christian organization.

When Christian parents pay $50,000 a year to send their children to a Christian college, they do not expect professors to deconstruct all that their children have learned from them and from their pastors. Yet that is precisely how some professors view their roles, as I learned from one administrator who called the first week "Unlearn Week" at one Christian university.

The good news is that some colleges and universities still strive for distinctively, inherently, and intentionally Christian values. The title of a book by Robert Benee, *Quality with Soul: How Six Premier Colleges and Universities Keep Faith with Their Religious Traditions*, demonstrates that some colleges are staying true to the values of the people who sacrificed so much to bring them into existence.

Dr. Everett Piper, president of Oklahoma Wesleyan University, states that when parents are exploring sending their children to college, desiring a truly *Christian* university, they need to request a meeting with the president and the dean of the religion department to ask them some questions. If they won't meet with you, don't send your children to that school.

Dr. Piper says to ask the president and the head of the religion department two questions: "What is your view of Scripture?" and "What is truth?" He continues, "If they don't answer you, it is not because they do not know. It is because they refuse to answer. Ask them if they believe the Bible is infallible and totally reliable. Ask them if they believe that objective truth (principles that are *always* true, for everyone, at all times) exists."[25] The answers to these questions are extremely important. The eternal soul of your child is at stake.

WHY ARE WE SURPRISED?

As government has become more secular at its core, and clearly hostile to Christian faith through the misapplied and redefined concept of "separation of church and state," it's only natural to expect

the most powerful tool for societal transformation—public school—
to become its weapon of choice.

Is this an overstatement? Consider this: What possible justification
can there be to violate a student's First Amendment rights of religious
expression and practice, to selectively restrict the right of free speech,
and to remove the freedom of assembly? It is only to remove any influence of Jesus Christ on that student's life. Not only that, but in violating the student's individual liberties as encoded in the Constitution,
the government is forcibly restraining that student from being the
example of salt and light he or she is called to be every day (Matthew
5:13–16), not just in church on Sunday.

Our nation's falling academic standing isn't because of a supposed
lack of funding at every level. To paraphrase Mark 8:36, what good
would it be if all the money in the world went to educate our children,
but they were to lose their very souls?

Our current educational system doesn't need a massive infusion
of new tax revenue; it needs to be rudely awakened to the fact that it
is consumed with anti-Christian bigotry. This blindness to the eternal
value of faith can only be for one purpose—to knowingly or unknowingly turn an impressionable child away from a faith that saves and
points to the ultimate accountability we will all face. Our nation
ignores this truth to its own detriment.

WHO SHOULD TEACH?

As Romans 13:1–6 and 1 Peter 2:14 clearly show, government is
instituted by God to maintain order through the application of justice
and to provide an environment for the growth of good. When government begins to assume the role of a god and take upon itself the
responsibility to educate its citizens in a worldview contrary to God's,
it has begun planting the seeds of its own inevitable destruction.

Biblically, the education and nurturing of children is the responsibility of parents. They are the ones to train their children in the way they should live their lives and what values to embrace (Proverbs 22:6); they are the ones to provide discipline and instruction in the Lord (Deuteronomy 4:9; Ephesians 6:4); they are the ones to encourage their children to seek out and understand the mysteries of the universe that point toward a Creator that is all-knowing, all-loving, and merciful (Proverbs 25:2). Public education can complement the parents' role by providing skill development ("adding one thing to another to find the scheme of things," Ecclesiastes 7:27), information, and factual understanding of the created order around us.

But ultimately, when government schools overtly denigrate or destroy the attractiveness of one's faith, or teach that it is of no importance by ignoring it altogether, schools contradict their reason to exist.

Parents, take ownership of your children's education. Now. And if you are a believer attending college—stand firm! You are on the front lines of the battleground of the warzone where worldviews collide and agendas infiltrate. Ask questions. Research for yourself. Dig deep in Scripture. Seek God's wisdom, and commit everything you do to prayer to the almighty God (1 Thessalonians 5:16), who will help you fend off those influences that intend you harm.

CHAPTER SEVEN

POLITICAL CORRECTNESS

*In this era of political correctness, some people seem
unaware that being squeamish about words can mean being
blind to realities.*[1]

—THOMAS SOWELL

Political correctness is tyranny with manners.[2]

—CHARLTON HESTON

I f you've been raised in the United States, you've heard the term
politically correct (PC). In fact, somewhere along the line you've
probably been accused of not being PC, being overly PC, or finally
becoming PC.

If a person is PC, he is careful not to use words, language, behavior, or even looks that might possibly offend someone else, their group, or even their cause. Sounds like plain old common courtesy, doesn't it? Unfortunately, that is not what PC is all about. It is truly a WMD, a weapon of mass *distraction*. PC-ness has become so pervasive in our culture, media, universities, and political discourse that facts and reason are inconsequential compared to the quick-fix, PC, verbal lashes that can so easily discredit or destroy anyone disagreeing with you.

For example, it's not PC to describe the destruction of an unborn child as murder. The PC phrase is "a woman's right to choose." Marriage is a *love* relationship between any number or combination of men and women, not an archaic commitment between one husband and one wife. Some changes in terminology are appropriate for accuracy, but in the world of PC, that is not the goal.

POLITICAL CORRECTNESS OR CONTROL

PC-ness is about control. Forcing people to use concocted terms defined by the political Left (progressives) obscures reality and purposefully creates confusion. It also puts people on the defensive by being constantly hyperconcerned about saying the wrong thing and being branded as a horrible, ignorant person. Terminology and perceived or imagined prejudice becomes the issue—not the subject at hand. That effect is intended to disarm any objective dealing with real issues, while making the problem the one who disagrees.

Not surprisingly, the promoters and users of PC tactics are those who typically hate biblical truth, traditional morality, sexual restraint, personal responsibility, the nuclear family, or any other concept based on transcendent, unchanging truth revealed by an almighty God for our society's good.

SOME HISTORICAL PERSPECTIVE

"Political correctness" has been in the making for about one hundred years thanks to Marxism, socialism, and secularism. In 1919, the Hungarian Marxist theoretician Georg Lukacs asked, "Who will save us from Western Civilization?"[3] Marxists across

Europe responded with a determination to overcome traditional Christian morality that embraced patriotism, religion, and family values. What emerged was an ingenious plan to demonize and eventually deconstruct Western civilization through promotion of anti-moral behaviors and replace it with Marxism.

As early as the 1930s, these planners were advocating the breakdown of traditional family by undermining sexual mores and calling for sexual liberation and—in the words of Herbert Marcuse—a society of "polymorphous perversity."[4] Erich Fromm, for example, argued masculinity and femininity were simply social constructs that could be socially changed (sounds like today's gender confusion).[5] They hoped to foster the idea that labor, productivity, and progress were not virtuous, and that hedonistic, human sensual happiness and leisure was a greater goal.

As World War II spread in Europe, many of those leading this mindset moved to our country. Conveniently, Sigmund Freud's humanistic psychosexual theories were used to encourage Baby Boomers to abandon traditional morality and question all authority structures they disliked. The concepts really began to flourish in the 1960s as a result of the Vietnam antiwar movement and the generational revolution in both drug and sexual freedoms. Those of us who remember those days heard phrases like, "Do your own thing," "Make love, not war," and "Don't trust anyone over thirty." In fact, "If it feels good, do it" became a license to indulge in anything that went against your parents' uptight moral hang-ups and traditional values relating to family, church, work, and even our government.

But this movement didn't stop at rejecting traditional, Judeo-Christian values. It became aggressively political to destroy and discredit our values in the public square. To succeed, a new weapon was unleashed: *tolerance*. It would become the new moral imperative, but it's not true tolerance at all. This emotional appeal to be open to other people's differences was simply a tactic used by the progressive Left to exploit Western Christianity's kindness. Tolerance very quickly morphed into acceptance—the relativist's dream. Once it became politically incorrect to claim a moral high ground, or to believe there really was such a thing as right and wrong, all who disagreed were the evil ones.

WHAT IS TOLERANCE?

The traditional definition of tolerance, to recognize and respect the beliefs and lifestyles of others without necessarily agreeing with them, changed to the definition being taught today—everyone's values and practices are equally valid and all truth claims are equal and demand endorsement.

Now firmly ensconced within the Democratic Party, as well as the mainstream media, much of the entertainment industry, and most of our universities, the progressive Left would use the new "liberating tolerance" to advance its own brand of intolerance. "Marcuse defines 'liberating tolerance' as intolerance for anything coming from the Right and tolerance for anything coming from the Left."[6] If you don't think so, dare to say the wrong thing, and you could have your life destroyed by the PC police, even if what you are saying is demonstrably factual and true.

Of course, this isn't a two-way street—it's open season for anyone to say any offensive thing they want about Christians and conservatives. Virtually nothing is too vile to be off-limits. Even equating Christianity with radical Islam is becoming common fare to discredit our faith and what we stand for.

If you dare call someone a sinner, or some behavior a sin, you will be labeled as a hateful bigot. Hate crime legislation makes some crimes worthy of more punishment because of the PC mindset, not the actual act itself. The natural consequence of this perversion of justice is pushing for the punishment of politically incorrect thoughts and speech, rather than a person's actual actions. This has already played out across our nation. If you don't want to participate in providing services for homosexual marriages[7] or to perform abortions against your will,[8] you can be fired, fined and/or forced to undergo re-education or sensitivity training to ensure you now think *correctly*.[9]

In November of 2008, Californians voted on Proposition 8, a fourteen-word statement defending natural, biblical one man–one woman marriage. During the months leading up to and following the election, those who held views consistent with the last five thousand years of human existence endured unending attacks—some verbal, some worse. Many of the e-mails or electronic messages that came in were peppered with expletives. I have a number of friends who do interviews as I do. We all experience the same thing any time we publicly defend morality: vile and vicious attacks via social media. The messages that pour in are vitriolic and hostile, demonstrating how demented and demonized the human mind can become. These people—so filled with hate—accuse *us* of being haters.

Approximately twenty thousand of us marched from the National Mall to the front of the Supreme Court in Washington, D.C., in support of traditional marriage. We had a permit that allowed us to gather on the steps of the Supreme Court. The radicals advocating for same-sex "marriage" did not. When we arrived at the Supreme Court, we were blocked from the steps by about two thousand of those radicals. We decided to continue marching *past* the Supreme Court and did so—until they blocked us there, as well. At that point we were forced to stop. We simply went to our knees and began praying.

After we stood, I found myself staring face-to-face with one of the protestors, our faces about eighteen inches apart. I looked at him. He looked at me. I continued looking at him. He continued looking at me. Finally he burst out loudly, "Shut up!" I responded quietly, "I never said anything."

Why was I hated? He did not know me. Why did he order me to "shut up"? I had not said anything. He hated truth. He hated the spirit

of God. Our values represented the sacred and holy truths that a
demonized person disdains.

WHAT ARE WE TO DO?

We can't allow ourselves to be intimidated into saying and doing
nothing. It would be easy to disengage from our culture and the issues
of the day and live a life without controversy. But even that can't happen. Cultural progressives will not be satisfied with silence; they want
total and full acceptance from us. In other words, they want a complete and unconditional surrender. That is the nature of spiritual
warfare; there is no peaceful coexistence. If we are followers of Christ,
we had better prepare ourselves for the battle (Ephesians 6:10–19).

By its nature, darkness can't stand to have any light around. By
our very nature, we are the light of Christ shining in the world. How
do we fulfill the imperative to be salt and light (Matthew 5:13–16) if
we go into a closet and hide from the world? How will we ever be
bold enough to share the Gospel with others as Matthew 28:19–20
commands if we are afraid of offending someone? Remember, we are
the aroma of Christ—to those who are perishing, we are the fragrance
of death, but to those who are being saved we are the fragrance of life
(2 Corinthians 2:14–16).

Am I saying we don't need to be sensitive or understanding of
those whom we want to influence? Of course not. Even Paul became
all things to all people in order to win some (1 Corinthians 9:19–23),
but in doing so, he never compromised the truth or bought into the
destructive lies of the world. The Bible says we will be held to account
for every careless word we speak (Matthew 12:36), thus we of all
people know it is important to be clear when we talk with others so
we do not create unnecessary offense. Colossians 4:6 says, "Let your
speech always be gracious, seasoned with salt, so that you may know
how you ought to answer each person."

There are things that all of us have carelessly said that make assumptions about other people. These generalizations can be inadvertently offensive to others, particularly if they have been the brunt of stereotyping over and over again. But we also need to be wise as serpents and gentle as doves (Matthew 10:16). We are to call evil what it is. Paul says in Ephesians 5:11, "Take no part in the unfruitful works of darkness, but instead expose them." God can take care of Himself, but we are to be His representatives while on earth and call out foolishness when it takes on the garb of truth. Political correctness is a weapon used to destroy the messenger of righteousness. We simply need God's boldness and the perseverance to speak the truth in love (Ephesians 4:15). We have a choice to be politically correct according to the world's pattern and standards, or biblically correct according to the Spirit of Christ.

Our spiritually renewed heart should long for the latter.

PART III

FAMILY AND LIFE ISSUES

CHAPTER EIGHT

MARRIAGE

And He (Jesus) answered and said, "Have you not read that He who created them from the beginning made them male and female, and said, 'For this reason a man shall leave his father and mother and be joined to his wife, and the two shall become one flesh'? So they are no longer two, but one flesh. What therefore God has joined together, let no man separate."

—MATTHEW 19:4–6

W hy should we care about marriage? What is the foundation of marriage? And why is marriage such a big deal to God? It's important to know at the start that the Bible

- *opens* in Genesis with a marriage—between a man and a woman;
- *closes* in Revelation with a wedding—between a groom and bride; and
- extols one man–one woman marriage *in between* in both the Old and New Testaments.

Nowhere is there any affirmation of homosexual marriage or of homosexual acts. In fact, the consistent teaching throughout Scripture is one man–one woman covenant marriage. Always.

THE FULL IMAGE OF GOD

God is neither male nor female. The Old Testament writers use gender-specific metaphors to describe the indescribable.

Sometimes, the words used to describe God are distinctly masculine, most obviously the usage of "Father" or "He." At other times the phrases used to depict God are feminine—terms like a breast-feeding, nursing mother (Psalms 131:2; Isaiah 49:15), giving birth (Deuteronomy 32:18), in labor (Isaiah 42:14), or a mother hen (Matthew 23:37).

But the fact is, God is neither a he nor a she. Nor is God some androgynous middle ground. In Genesis 17:1 God's name is the Hebrew phrase *El Shaddai*. It is believed that *el* means mighty like a mountain, thus the strength of masculinity. *Shaddai* likely comes from the Hebrew word for breast, such as feeding a newborn baby, thus the nurturing feminine characteristic. That single name for God includes the full spectrum of masculinity and femininity.

We are made in His image. However, a male alone cannot fully represent all of the descriptors of the image of God. For example, a male, by himself, cannot manifest the full spectrum of God's features historically associated with femininity (tenderness). Thus, no husband can represent the full image of God. At the same time, a female, alone, cannot do justice to His image either, due to a lack of classic masculine strength.

In spite of the fact that we are created by God individually, *we express the fullest image of God only when the two halves of humanity complement each other and become one.*

"ADAM" THE MAN VS. "ADAM" AS HUMANKIND

Let's go deeper into the Hebrew language of Genesis. The traditional view of human creation is that God created Adam, put him to sleep, took a rib, and created Eve. But the Old Testament was originally written in Hebrew, not English. Is the Hebrew text saying that God created Adam, a male, and then created Eve, a female, from Adam's rib? I think there is something more profound in the Hebrew Old Testament that reveals a deeper understanding of the Genesis account.

In the beginning, God created not Adam the male, but *adam*, that is, humankind. Don't picture Adam the male. The word *adam*, pronounced "awh-DAHM," means humankind or personhood. It is later that Adam is the name of a male. But initially God created *adam*—small *a*—that is, humankind.

After creating humankind, God said, "It is not good that *adam*—humankind—is alone." This was not a case of God creating a male and then saying, "It is not good that a male is alone, so I will make a female." That is not what happened.

I suggest a more correct reading of the Hebrew would be, "It is not good for humankind to be *at one*." Let's not miss the point. God made humankind. He then said, "It is not good for humankind to be *at one* or *one*—or to live *in solitude*."

Here we have the "splitting of the *adam*," so to speak, as *adam*, or humankind, gets split apart. We end up with male and female.

But what about the proverbial rib? The word *rib* does not appear in the ancient Hebrew text. The word that is there is *tsela*. What is *tsela*? It can be translated *half* or *side*. Don't miss the significance of this next sentence. Instead of God creating Adam and taking his rib to create Eve, the text says that God created humankind, observed it was not good for humankind to be one, or alone, and then took a side or a half of humankind and created a female (Eve). What remained was male (Adam). In other words, the whole (humanity) that was created in the full image of God (with both the strength of masculin-ity and the tenderness of femininity) is now the two complementary halves of humanity: male and female.

One of the reasons for the strong sexual attraction of males and females to each other is the desire for the two halves of humanity to come back together—undoing the "splitting of the *adam*"—and reunit-ing male and female as halves to make a whole, now reflecting the full image of God. But let's take this exciting concept one step further.

ISH AND *ISHAH*: *YOD* AND *HEY*

The Hebrew word for man is *ish*. The Hebrew word for woman is *ishah*, pronounced "i-SHAH." Here is the difference between *ish* and *ishah*:

- In the Hebrew language, there is one Hebrew letter in *ish* (man) that is not in *ishah* (woman), and that is the Hebrew letter *yod*.
- In the Hebrew word for *ishah* (woman), there is one Hebrew letter that is not in *ish* (man), and that is the Hebrew letter *hey*.

Yod and *hey* form the basis for the word Yahweh or YHWH, the name for God that is used 6,800 times in the Old Testament. In other words, when you put ish (man) and ishah (woman) together, you have yod-hey or Yahweh or God—the expression of the full image of God. Even the Hebrew words for man and woman depict this breathtaking construct.

Let's be clear: two men do not have the image of God. Two women do not have the image of God. Only a man and a woman—covenant-ally (permanently) joined—offer that spectacular reality and imagery.

THE COMPLEMENTARITY OF MALE AND FEMALE

When the two complementary halves of humanity unite—physically, spiritually, mentally, emotionally, and psychologically—the image of God, containing both tenderness and strength, is manifested. Male and female are created anatomically, emotionally, and spiritually for oneness.

In what way is the male-female union a depiction of God? In sexual union, husband and wife become co-creators, in a sense, with God. Children come into being as husband and wife unite. A sperm and an egg unite to form (miraculously) a human. A person! Male and female becoming one is what Genesis establishes as the components for this image. Science knows *that* an egg and a sperm unite to create a human. But science cannot explain *how* or *why* it happens.

This is but one of the reasons the Bible does not affirm homosexual marriage nor the homosexual act. Nowhere. Not overtly. Not covertly.

JESUS' STATEMENTS

The only time Jesus participated in a wedding or spoke of marriage, he referred to male and female constituents. Jesus stated unequivocally, "A man will leave his father and mother and be united to his wife, and the two will become one flesh. So they are no longer two, but one" (Matthew 19:5–6a, NIV). Once again, we see complementarity.

And to assure no one ever was tempted to tamper with the definition of marriage, Jesus added, "What I have defined, let no Supreme Court ever redefine!" Yes, that is the "Loose Garlow Translation." Jesus actually said, "What God has joined together, let no one separate" (Matthew 19:6, NIV).

MARRIAGE IN REVELATION

As important as this issue is of manifesting the image of God, there is an even greater, deeper role for marriage. In the book of Revelation, the writer speaks of the marriage banquet of Jesus and the Church. Here is my question: Did God look down on earth, see marriage, and borrow the imagery to describe Jesus as the groom and the Church as the bride?

Often we think real marriage is that which we see here on earth. We sometimes assume that God simply borrowed the metaphor to describe what will happen at the culmination of all history, the marriage of Jesus and the Church. But in reality, we have it backward.

The real Marriage is the one at the culmination of history, the Marriage of the Groom (Jesus) and the Bride (the Church). Thus we have never seen the *real* Marriage. That is yet to come—at the end of time. Here on earth, we only have a shadow of the real thing. With earthly marriage, we are experiencing merely the *hors d'oeuvre*, not the main course. God established earthly marriage between a man and a woman to provide a tiny glimpse of the spectacular true Marriage to come. Intimacy between a married man and woman is only a miniscule glimpse of the breathtaking oneness that Jesus and the Church will experience.

Think of the greatest marriage you can. (If you are married, I hope that is your marriage.) Yet the greatest marriage—spelled with a small *m*—does not compare to the indescribable Marriage—spelled with a capital *M*—that will take place between Jesus, the Son of God, and the Church.

Do you understand this—the whole idea of Jesus and the Church being married? I confess I cannot fully grasp it. And Paul knew that. That is why in Ephesians 5, after talking about marriage of a man and a woman, Paul suddenly stated, "This is a profound mystery, but I am talking about Christ and the church" (Ephesians 5:32). He is clarifying that he wasn't ultimately talking about earthly marriages, but was using that to try to understand the Marriage of Jesus and the Church.

We even used marital-bed language to depict this event—the closure of history. We sometimes call it the *consummation* or the *climax* of history. How interesting.

WHY THE DEFINITION MATTERS

And that is why people of understanding defend traditional, historic, biblical, natural orthodox marriage (male-female).

It is not ultimately about earthly marriage or even about the practice of homosexuality as such. It is about the desire to preserve the magnificent picture of the image of God. It is about His ultimate design for the Cosmos—the Grand Wedding of His Son to the Prepared Bride. And that is why the definition of marriage—as between a man and woman—matters. To you. To our nation. To God.

THE LEGAL CASE FOR MARRIAGE

Thirty-one states voted for marriage to be defined as between one man and one woman.[1] Only three states (Maine, Maryland, and Washington)—where anti-marriage forces outspent those for biblical marriage by up to 10 to 1—voted to decimate the global and historic definition of marriage.

Then on June 26, 2015, the U.S. Supreme Court forced a non-historic definition of marriage on the entire nation.[2] The five unelected majority justices gave an opinion that flies in the face of all historic data, social science, and the conviction of all the world's religions. The Constitution never mentions marriage. All items not listed in the Constitution automatically fall under the authority of individual states.

In the year 2000, California residents voted for Proposition 22, which consisted of fourteen words ("Only marriage between a man and a woman is valid and recognized in California") added to the family code of the state of California.[3] But by 2007, when it became apparent that law might be thrown out by activist judges, the entire state voted again—this time for those same words to be placed in the California Constitution. Proposition 22 was, in fact, thrown out by the California Supreme Court on May 15, 2008.[4]

Consequently, in 2008 Proposition 8 was put on the ballot in California. As the race heated up, a poll indicated at one point that Proposition 8 was behind 38 percent to 55 percent. Never in the history of California had a proposition started below 50 percent and won.[5] Each side of the debate raised approximately $40 million.[6] When the vote was completed, one man–one woman marriage won 52.3 percent with 7 million votes.[7] The California Supreme Court later upheld this Proposition 8 language defining marriage in California.[8]

But Proposition 8 was then struck down by a federal court judge in San Francisco[9] and then by the U.S. Court of Appeals for the Ninth Circuit.[10] Later it was taken to the U.S. Supreme Court. At their inaugurations, California's governor and attorney general swore under oath to defend the California Constitution. Yet they chose to violate their oaths.[11] Consequently, the people of California rose up, raised the money and sent attorneys to argue the case before the Supreme Court of the United States. Contrary to popular belief, the Supreme Court never ruled on the merit of Proposition 8. They did, however, rule that the people of California who defended marriage did not have legal standing to argue the case before the Supreme Court.[12]

Ironically, this law is still part of the California Constitution, though it's being violated every day. Article 1, Section 7.5, still states those fourteen words: "Only marriage between a man and a woman is valid and recognized in California."[13]

CHAPTER NINE

SCHOOL CHOICE AND PARENTAL AUTHORITY

The best means of forming a manly, virtuous, and happy people will be found in the right education of youth. Without this foundation, every other means, in my opinion, must fail.[1]

—GEORGE WASHINGTON, LETTER TO GEORGE CHAPMAN, DECEMBER 15, 1784

He who knows most knows how little he knows.

—THOMAS JEFFERSON

My late wife and I adopted four children. When one of my sons was in third grade, he was to receive special counseling from a public school. I informed the counselor that I would sit in on the session. He promptly informed me that I would not. A discussion ensued.

I asked, "To whom does the child belong, the parents or the state (meaning government and government schools)?" He paused, feeling a bit trapped, not wanting to say, *the state*, but chafing at the idea of conceding the point by saying, *the parents*.

He chose to answer what he *thought* I wanted to hear. He answered softly and a bit begrudgingly, "The parents."

"Wrong," I responded. "Children do not *belong* to parents *or* the state." He seemed relieved, thinking we had discovered a middle ground. I continued, "Children belong to God. He made them. But He has entrusted them to parents for the first twenty years or so of their lives until they are able to make life work on their own. So as the one to whom God has given this child, I insist on remaining in the room if you, a complete stranger to me and my child, are going to have input into my child's thinking."

He refused to allow me to stay. Consequently, I graciously refused his counseling for my child, and we left. I have no regrets about that decision. This scenario repeated itself with other counselors in later years, and is a familiar situation for many parents.

Why on earth would the culture be so anti-parent? Because they—the state or the counselor—think they know better than we do as parents. Some of them are convinced we are buffoons. We don't know anything. After all, have we gone through all the courses that they have? No. So we need to be quiet and let the experts talk.

THE ULTIMATE EDUCATOR AND PROTECTOR

Now let me be clear. We had positive interactions with 99 percent of our children's teachers. But we certainly ran into the above attitude on occasion, and we have had too many of our friends encounter this attitude among educators, occasionally with catastrophic results.

My wife and I have had our children in public schools, private schools, Christian schools, charter schools, home schooling and in "non-public placement" schools. Frankly, we have had great relationships with almost all of them. We have had remarkable teachers.

But there were times we had to be firm with some counselors or administrators by saying, "We are the parents. We are the ones making decisions for our children and their well-being. You will invest in them for a short time, and we appreciate it. But we have invested in them since they were born (or adopted), and we will be with them until we die or until they die, whichever comes first. I would take a bullet for my children. You likely would not, nor do I expect you to. So we plan to be involved in our children's lives and direct their education journey because (1) we revere God and He will hold us accountable some day for how we raised them, and (2) we will do anything to see them established as strong, godly, productive citizens who experience *the joy of learning* and make it a lifelong passion." Structured education is not an end in itself. The goal of formal education is to help people fall in love with learning, to experience *the joy of learning*, so they will become life-long learners.

The American contemporary statist (meaning state-owned and state-run) educational system has it totally wrong. The children belong to God, and God has designated parents—and parents only—to guide their education process. Those parents may contract with tutors or teachers to aid in their children's critical educational journey.

Although we had great experiences with all the forms of schooling mentioned above, we were partial to home schooling. Why? Because home schooling taught us how, as parents, *to turn every event into a joyous and invigorating learning experience*. It stirred the inquisitive nature within us, for parents and students alike. In fact, we were able to actually live out the Deuteronomy 6:7; 11:19 mandate to instill knowledge, truth, life lessons, reasoning ability, and even practical skills into our children throughout the day, making all of life a teachable moment.

It was not our degrees that made us good home schooling parents; it was our passion for making education fun and exciting. If school officials, administrators, teachers, and board members realize that the children belong to God and have been entrusted to parents, the learning environment shifts from surviving to thriving. The American model and culture has it backwards. The state is not the ultimate educator and protector of my child. The parents are.

THE PARENT AS PRIMARY EDUCATOR AND GUARDIAN

According to the title of Hillary Clinton's book, our society would like us to believe that "it takes a village" to raise a child. A village *does* play a role. But it does *not* supplant the role of the parent. As Christians, we are called to teach our children diligently in the way they should go, in the principles and truth of God's Word. Psalms 127:3 says children are a reward from Him—a blessing and a gift. This blessing is entrusted to parents, not the village, and with that stewardship comes a great responsibility:

- Proverbs 22:6: "Train up a child in the way he should go, and when he is old he will not depart from it" (NKJV).
- Deuteronomy 6:6–7: "And these words that I command you today shall be on your heart. You shall teach them diligently to your children, and shall talk of them when you sit in your house, and when you walk by the way, and when you lie down, and when you rise" (NKJV).
- 3 John 1:4: "I have no greater joy than to hear that my children are walking in the truth."

Parents have a responsibility to train their children in the ways of righteousness as Ephesians 6:4 says. That responsibility includes discipline, instruction, training, and education. However, we have an educational system in America that often strips parents of rights and choices.

ELIMINATION OF PARENTAL RIGHTS

Allow me to give a most bizarre example. When I took my two daughters to get their ears pierced at an appropriate age, I had to sign forms.[2] Yet in my state, those same two daughters could have an extremely serious medical procedure—an abortion—without my even knowing it.[3]

Today, thirty-eight states require minors' parents to be notified when receiving an abortion,[4] which means in twelve states parents have no right to even be notified when their minor child receives an abortion. And in some states, children can actually undergo a sex-change operation as early as fifteen years of age, paid for by the state, *without any parental consent.*[5]

The Departments of Health and Human Services and Education recently drafted a potential government policy statement on family engagement, and they sum it up better than any number of examples would: "It is the position of the Departments [of HHS and Education] that all early childhood programs and schools recognize families as *equal partners* (italics added) in improving children's development, learning and wellness across all settings, and over the course of their children's developmental and educational experiences."[6]

Notice, "equal partners." The government believes they have *equal rights* with the parent to care for the child! The underlying reasoning behind these new laws and statements removing parental authority is that the state and popular culture believe they know how to raise the child better than the parent.

This flies in the face of what Scripture teaches: that children are to submit in obedience to the parents and parents are called to give an account to God for those entrusted to them.

Colossians 3:20 states, "Children, obey your parents in everything, for this pleases the Lord." And truth be told, with our public education system becoming more and more antithetical to Christian values and biblical principles, it's becoming a tangible example of 2 Timothy 3:7. These expert educators are "always learning and never able to come to the knowledge of the truth." No wonder Scripture is quite clear; parents are to be the primary educators and equippers of their children and have the right and obligation to do so: "Listen my son, to your father's instruction and do not forsake your mother's teaching" (Proverbs 1:8).

One of the areas with the greatest infringement on parental rights is the American educational system.

EROSION OF PARENTAL RIGHTS

This decline in parental involvement can be traced back to the early 1900s and a man named John Dewey, credited as the father of progressive education. Dewey was one of the authors of the Humanist Manifesto.[7] Embracing humanism, he denied the existence of a creator and lawgiver and supported the beliefs of global government and world relativism. He was a key player in the founding of the National Education Association (NEA) and established much of the liberal doctrine it adheres to today (seen in the political candidates and policies it supports).[8]

Dewy focused on the relationship between the individual and society. He developed a school curriculum that emphasized the child instead of the subject matter.[9] Focus was equally distributed between the learning process and what was learned. You might be thinking, *Well that sounds good, right?* While it looks good in theory, it has had devastating consequences. It overturned traditional education, which placed all the emphasis on what was learned and not on a child-centered classroom.

Traditional education valued faith in a creator, moral absolutes, right and wrong, strict discipline, and hard work. However, these values knowingly or unknowingly were gradually cast aside as the focus on the child grew. The classroom became more about what the child thought was right and wrong rather than absolutes, and more concerned about protecting a child's fragile self-esteem than solid subject matter learning.[10]

DEPARTMENT OF EDUCATION

It gets worse. Roughly eighty years following John Dewey's first education methods were established, the American Department of Education was formed. A cabinet level department, with the secretary of education at its head, appointed by the president, President Jimmy Carter signed this new department into law in 1979.[11]

According to the Department of Education website, the DoED's mission is to "serve America's students—to promote student achievement and preparation for global competitiveness by fostering educational excellence and ensuring equal access."[12]

While well-intentioned, this government-run department has stolen power from parents and local authority and, instead, created a federally directed education system. One of the purposes of the department is "to increase the accountability of Federal education programs to the President, the Congress and the public."[13]

SCHOOL CHOICE

In addition to the removal of biblically founded character training in schools, another reason why America is failing its children is a lack of educational choices and equal opportunity. We have an educational system that discriminates against the single mother and the poor, by limiting options. It's a system that allows wealth to determine a child's education. If you are fortunate enough to buy a home in a good school district, your child has a better chance of receiving a strong education. However, if you cannot afford to live in a good district or pay for a private school, you have no choice but to send your child to the school located in your neighborhood, even if it's a poor performing school.

In America, we have a free-market economy that is beginning to adopt more choices, but that hasn't always been the case when it comes to education. Thankfully, parents' desire for quality education and choices for their children has led to the development of other options: charter schools and home schooling.

Charter schools began in the early 1990s as a variation of the public school system. These schools provide the educators extensive freedom from many of the regulations found in traditional public schools. Parents can choose what school best fits their child's needs and interests. We now have charter schools that specialize in science, mathematics, technology, the arts, or other fields of interest.

Currently 2.75 million students attend charter schools in the United States.[14] In the last ten years we have seen charter school enrollment increase by 225 percent and the number of charter schools increase by a whopping 118 percent.[15] The demand has become so great that school acceptance depends on a lottery system; thousands of children are placed on waiting lists.[16] In California in the 2012–2013 school year, over forty-nine thousand students were placed on a waiting list, with fifteen thousand waiting students in Los Angeles alone.[17]

The demand is great because it's a sliver of opportunity and one choice closer to a free-market education system. The suffocating restraint of the teachers' unions is slowly being broken, giving parents the right to be, well, parents.

There is, however, another choice for parents who are able to stay home with their children to provide in-home education. Parents can find a wide variety of solid curricula, as well as home schooling organizations nationwide that are incredibly well-equipped to help ensure their child is adequately educated in a Christian worldview with the skills to tackle the challenges they will face in their lives.

We've allowed ourselves, as parents, to be bumped from the "table." We've allowed policy makers, school administrators, and self-interested teachers' unions to decide what's best for our children. This needs to change.

CHAPTER TEN

ABORTION

*I've noticed that everyone who is for abortion
has already been born.*[1]

—RONALD REAGAN

I go on Facebook from time to time. I posted a story once that produced over 18,000 "shares," and more than 71,000 "likes." Why? The story touched a nerve. Allow me to explain.

Angela grew up in the Midwest. After she had just turned fourteen years old, she was flattered that two high school seniors wanted to take her to a movie. However, instead of going to a movie, they drove the truck into a field in the darkness of night and there they raped her. Several months later, a doctor confirmed her pregnancy, and the decision was made to place the baby for adoption.

Angela's pregnancy was problematic. The closest hospital that could assist such a complicated pregnancy was sixty miles away. Her alcoholic father and mother were raising four other children, including two toddlers, and could not come to see her. For several months, the fourteen-year-old lay flat on her back, by herself, in a large city a long way from her small town. Finally, the baby was born—a girl. My late wife and I adopted her. We named that baby girl Janie.

Thirty-six years later, my wife Carol died of cancer. We buried her in California in a cemetery near our home, but we also had a memorial service for her in Kansas. As the service ended for my wife, we attended a reception for family and friends, hosted by my cousin at his farmhouse. It was there that our daughter Janie was able to talk with the doctor who had, thirty-six years earlier, cared for Janie's birthmother. As a result of that conversation, Janie began a process that resulted in her talking with her birthmother by phone and eventually meeting her face-to-face.

It was as they talked that Janie learned her birthmother had been raped. In the thirty-six years of Janie's life, we had always felt such gratitude toward this woman whom we'd never met, but who had made such a great sacrifice. Becoming aware of the component of rape and her young age caused our already immense gratitude toward her to skyrocket.

My Facebook post—shared with the permission of Janie—contained only portions of the information I just shared with you. But it resonated with tens of thousands of people.

Why? The pathos of the story. A baby was saved. A scared fourteen-year-old was remarkably brave and sacrificial. A baby grew up to become a truly amazing woman of God today. What the enemy meant for evil, God has turned for good (Genesis 50:20). And birthmother Angela is our hero. We honor her. We praise God for her.

GOD'S VIEW

Let's cut to the chase. What does God say about when life begins? This is one of those political or social issues about which the Bible is crystal clear. God's Word clearly reveals how He values pre-born life:

- Psalms 139:13–16: "For you created my inmost being; you knit me together in my mother's womb. I praise you because I am fearfully and wonderfully made; your works are wonderful; I know that full well. My frame was not hidden from you when I was made in the secret place. When I was woven together in the depths of the earth, your eyes saw my unformed body. All the days ordained for me were written in your book before one of them came to be."

- Jeremiah 1:4–5: "The word of the Lord came to me, saying, "Before I formed you in the womb I knew you, before you were born I set you apart; I appointed you as a prophet to the nations."

- Genesis 25:22–23: "The children struggled together within her, and she said, 'If it is thus, why is this happening to me?' So she went to inquire of the Lord. And the Lord said to her, 'Two nations are in your womb, and two peoples from within you shall be divided; the one shall be stronger than the other, the older shall serve the younger.'"

- Psalms 22:10: "From birth I was cast on you; from my mother's womb you have been my God."

- Luke 1:44: "As soon as the sound of your greeting reached my ears, the baby in my womb leaped for joy."

How could it be any clearer than that? There is no Bible verse saying an embryo only becomes a living soul at the second or third trimester.

Old Testament Scripture actually places a greater emphasis on the protection of life for a pregnant woman than for others in society. Exodus 21:22–23 states, "If people are fighting and hit a pregnant woman and she gives birth prematurely but there is no serious injury, the offender must be fined whatever the woman's husband demands and the court allows. But if there is serious injury, you are to take life for life." This was the law God established through Moses. Why was it so serious to place a pregnant woman in harm? Because it was not just one life, but two at risk.

The same people who say, *it is merely a blob of tissue*, are quick to condemn and sue a car company for killing a *baby* when a woman and her pre-born child are killed in a car crash. If a man shoots and kills a pregnant woman, he can be charged with killing the mother and the baby. When a doctor diagnoses a woman as pregnant, he doesn't say, "You're going to have a fetus." He says, "You're going to have a baby." In all these scenarios, the truth remains constant: from the moment of conception, life exists.

Abortion kills a human being. Watching the daily news and the executions of innocent Christian men, women, and children by ISIS and other Islamic groups is heart-wrenching. Equally horrific are the murderous actions happening to the unborn in our communities. Every single day in America, innocent blood runs under the streets of our cities. And what does God say about this?

- Proverbs 24:11–12: "Rescue those being led away to death; hold back those staggering toward slaughter. If you say, 'But we knew nothing about this,' does not he who weighs the heart perceive it? Does not he who guards your life know it? Will he not repay each person according to what he has done?"

Allow me to rewind that, this time with another version, The Living Translation:

- Proverbs 24:11–12: "Rescue those who are unjustly sentenced to death; don't stand back and let them die. Don't try to disclaim responsibility by saying you didn't know about it. For God, who knows all hearts, knows yours, and He knows you knew! And He will reward everyone according to his deeds."

Approximately 50,000,000 abortions occur globally each year. That means a shocking 140,000 people are killed daily, 5,700 each hour, nearly 100 every minute, almost 2 every second.[2] Approximately 1.5 million abortions occur annually in the U.S., one of the highest rates of any developed country. That means that 4,100 babies are murdered daily in the U.S., 177 every hour, 3 every minute. We have to wonder—with each life given a purpose from God—what might they have accomplished that could have made this world a better place?

UNWANTED PREGNANCY?

Does it have to be this way? No! When my daughter Janie was about twelve years of age, we lived in the heart of the Dallas-Ft. Worth area, Texas. The Tarrant County (Ft. Worth) Commissioners, led by Judge Tom Vandergriff, a former congressman, held a hearing on whether or not to allow abortions at the John Peter Smith County Hospital. Twelve-year-old Janie was one of the final speakers of the day, and closed her remarks with the words, "I may have been an unwanted pregnancy, but I am a very wanted child!" Vandergriff said that in his years in Congress he had never heard a better speech than hers.

The point is this: when birth mothers feel they cannot care for a baby, many others stand ready to adopt. It is not necessary to kill the child. Some estimate that there might be as many as two million parents across America waiting to adopt.

What if the baby will be deformed? That makes no difference to many prospective parents. I recall one Saturday I had gone with a group of people to one of the Dallas-Ft. Worth killing centers to pray that the spirit of death would not prevail. A young birthmother arrived, ready to have an abortion because she had learned her baby would be horribly deformed. We asked her if she would be willing for the baby to be lovingly adopted by caring parents. She said yes. We placed one call; the baby survived and was placed into the arms of a couple who loved the child.

IS A FETUS REALLY A HUMAN BEING?

Is a fetus really a life? According to science, and common sense, even the earliest human embryo is biologically alive. It fulfills all four of the scientific criteria needed to establish biological life: metabolism, growth, reaction to stimuli, and reproduction. In fact, all the genetic material that is needed to fully define and mature this human being is already present from the point of conception.

Consider these realities:

- Eighteen days after conception a baby's heart begins to beat with its own blood.
- Twenty-eight days from conception a baby has eyes and ears.
- At forty-two days the baby has brain waves.
- At ten weeks babies can feel pain and even have developed tiny fingernails.
- Babies have been born and have survived at only twelve weeks.[3]

Despite incredible scientific advancement in monitoring the growth of a baby in the womb, the killing of unborn babies continues as our culture becomes more and more hardened to the reality of the life inside its mother. Look at America's calloused condition:

- When we discovered the so-called fetus had a heart-beat—we did not stop killing.
- When sonograms were developed allowing us to physically see the form of a baby—we did not stop killing.
- When Jane Roe from the Supreme Court case *Roe v. Wade*, which legalized abortion through the third trimester, came out explaining she never actually had an abortion and admitted the case was the "biggest mistake of her life"—we still did not stop killing. Roe said in a television ad, "You read about me in history books, but now I am dedicated to spreading the truth about preserving the dignity of all human life from natural conception to natural death."[4] When she came out against abortion—we did not stop killing.
- When abortion was exposed through the Silent Scream documentary in 1984—we did not stop killing.
- When Planned Parenthood began dismembering post-aborted babies' body parts and selling them for profit—we did not stop killing.

What will it take? Are we as numb as Nazi Germany when six million—some say eight million—men, women, and children were marched off to gas chambers? As a nation, we have ignored every ounce of science and turned our backs on millions of dying people.

IS ABORTION OKAY WHEN THE MOTHER'S LIFE IS AT RISK?

Performing an abortion to save the life of the mother is one of the most popular comebacks against pro-life arguments; yet this circumstance makes up only 0.118 percent—that is 1/10 of 1 percent—of all abortions in the U.S.[5] This is the only scenario different from all the others, because in this situation the choice is between saving one life, the mother's, or losing two lives, mother's and baby's. In reality, both lives are made in the image of God (Genesis 1:27) and worthy to be protected with whatever means medically made available. It is *extraordinarily* rare to have to take the life of the unborn child to ensure the mother lives. Even in this case, God is sovereign over both lives and does not grant any arbitrariness over when life is to be taken (1 Samuel 2:6).

IS ABORTION OKAY IN THE CASES OF RAPE AND INCEST?

Killing a child because of the circumstances of its conception is not biblical.

Deuteronomy 24:16 states, "Fathers are not to be put to death for their children, nor children put to death for their fathers; each will die for their own sin." Killing the child because of someone else's crime is wrong and can never be justified. What is the crime that the child has committed that deserves death? Taking the innocent life of a child because of the sin of a parent is committing an even worse sin, one that can never be rectified. We also need to realize that abortions due to rape and incest make up only about 1 percent of all abortions.[6] Ninety-nine percent of abortions have nothing to do with these extreme or severe situations.[7]

MORAL STANDARDS VIOLATED

Two key moral standards must be recognized in order to protect human life. We are all familiar with the first—the Sixth Commandment in Exodus 20:13, "You shall not murder." The second moral standard is found in Psalms 139, "You knit me together in my mother's womb." Human life begins at conception and therefore has all rights to life.

When these standards no longer carry weight with our leaders, religious liberty suffers. The Affordable Care Act passed in 2010 requires religious organizations to provide contraceptives, and later mandated abortion-inducing drugs.[8] Even before the new healthcare law, there had been cases of forced abortion participation in the medical field. At Mount Sinai Hospital in New York, a nurse was forced to aid in a non-emergency abortion procedure even though the hospital knew it violated her religious beliefs.[9] The irony: the hospital that forced the nurse to perform the abortion is called Mount Sinai, which is the location where the Lord God commanded, "Thou shalt not murder!"

LIFE IS WINNING THE DEBATE

The millennial generation is becoming pro-life despite the culture's failure to protect life. Back in the 1990s, 34 percent of millennials thought abortion should remain legal in all situations.[10] However, by 2010, only 22 percent wanted to keep abortion legal in all cases,[11] so with the 2 percent who were undecided, this means that 76 percent of millennials oppose keeping abortion legal in all cases.[12] The millennial generation is more pro-life than their parents' generation.

Perhaps millennials should be credited for the changes in abortion statistics. According to the National Right to Life calculations of abortions, the numbers are actually declining from 1.6 million abortions performed in 1990.[13] Today it estimates the abortion numbers have fallen to 1.2 million annually.[14] This is still a heart-wrenching number—but fewer deaths, nevertheless.

I have taken people on church history tours of Europe that include a stop at Buchenwald, one of Germany's concentration camps. My wife has visited Auschwitz in Poland. Children walk in utter disbelief through these horrific sites today and ask their grandparents and great-grandparents, "Where were you? What were you doing to stop this?" Someday, there will be tours of abortuaries, the killing centers in the United States. Children will look at their parents, grandparents, and great-grandparents and demand an explanation: *Where were you when this genocide happened? What did you do to stop it?*

CHAPTER ELEVEN

SEXUAL ORIENTATION AND GENDER IDENTITY

I didn't want to be a boy. I kind of wanted to be nothing. I don't relate to what people would say defines a girl or a boy, and I think that's what I had to understand: Being a girl isn't what I hate, it's the box that I get put into.[1]

—MILEY CYRUS, SINGER AND FORMER DISNEY CHANNEL STAR

"I've gone back to being a child," says a fifty-year-old Canadian man, formerly known as Paul Wolscht, who was married and the father of seven children. He now claims he is a six-year-old little girl named Stefonknee. He has been adopted by a "mommy and a daddy" and spends his days with a coloring book.[2]

Miley Cyrus isn't the only one who doesn't want to be put into a box as her gender. Facebook has now broadened their sex and gender setting preferences from two choices, male and female, to over fifty-six choices, which now includes the option to list up to ten gender nomenclatures on one's Facebook profile.[3]

In 2015, Bruce Jenner, who now calls himself Caitlyn Jenner, boosted the transgender cause with his transition, announcing it on

Diane Sawyer's show,[4] making the cover of *Vanity Fair*,[5] accepting the Arthur Ashe courage award at the ESPYS,[6] and being named by *Glamour* magazine as the 2015 Woman of the Year.[7] Bruce Jenner has vowed to do anything to help "reshape the landscape of how transgender people are viewed and treated."[8] And in 2015 we witnessed him accomplishing just that.

SEXUAL ORIENTATION

Defining one's sexual orientation is a modern phenomenon. In fact, it was not until 1911 that the word *homosexual* was used in a medical journal.[9] Prior to that, the practice of homosexual behavior had a simple name: sin.

Prior to sonograms, the gender of a baby was not known until birth. If you were born in that era, the first phrase likely said about you was, *It's a boy*, or, *It's a girl*. At that moment, you ceased being an *it* and you became a *he* or a *she*. Oh, if things could return to that honest simplicity. But that is not to be.

The Merriam-Webster Dictionary defines gender as, "the state of being male or female."[10] And according to *Merriam-Webster*, a person's sex is also defined as, "the state of being male or female."[11] So sex and gender are exactly the same? Well, it depends on whom you ask. While the two terms might still be defined identically in the dictionary, other sources claim that since science is improving, the terms are actually evolving.[12]

The Daily Beast says a person's sex refers mainly to, "biology and is a configuration of chromosomes, hormones, gonads (ovaries, testicles), reproductive units (sperm, egg), and internal and external anatomy" (a standard dictionary defintion).[13] The Daily Beast then goes further: "And while sex is often talked about as if the only two options are male and female, this two-sex system is inadequate for understanding the sex characteristics of all people."[14]

They go on to define gender as "the personal sense of who you are."[15]

Thus while sex may refer to one's biological plumbing, gender refers to how you feel that day. In an interview with *Paper* magazine, Miley Cyrus described herself as "gender-fluid,"[16] meaning she has different gender identities at different times, sometimes even multiple gender identities at once, and sometimes none at all. Are you confused? You are not alone.

IMPLICATIONS OF "YOU WERE BORN THAT WAY"

Having muddied the waters with a plethora of perversion, we need to ask, *were they born that way?* If you believe that they were, then what right do you have to change how they were born? And if they were not born that way, can they change?

Dr. Jennifer Roback Morse, a biblically alert thinker, writing in *Crisis Magazine*, noted, "In fact, the significance of that phrase, 'born that way,' can vary considerably. For one person, it may be the truth as he experiences it. For another, it may be a permission slip to engage in behavior he could not justify otherwise."[17]

Morse continues, "What do these beliefs have in common? The idea that there is one and only one valid form of expression for each person who experiences same-sex attraction is a form of moral determinism that robs the person of meaningful choices. Likewise, the 'Born That Way' belief suggests that once a person discovers an inkling of same-sex attraction, he need not engage in any further moral deliberation."[18]

Because of the pressure of present culture, any person who is wondering if he or she is "born that way," a euphemism for homosexuality (or some other deviance from heterosexuality), better not consider being anything but homosexual, in behavior and self-description. In other words, the movement coerces people away from thinking they might not have to identify as homosexual.

This is not just imagination. This has actually happened to—that is, *was forced on*—one of the pastors of the church where I serve as senior pastor. Our counseling pastor is certified as a marriage and family therapist. But in a recent lawsuit with the State of California bearing his name which he lost, he, and all the other counselors in our state, cannot now legally tell a minor he or she *does not have to be* homosexual![19] Our pastor is forced to remain silent on the capacity of a person to possibly *not* act as a homosexual! Talk about loss of First Amendment rights!

It should be noted that there is no credible scientific evidence that one is "born that way." The causes of homosexuality—or other variant forms of sexual preference—are not known with certainty. But identical twin studies, in which one twin is homosexual and the other twin is heterosexual, clearly indicate the "born that way" argument has no merit.[20]

Another hotbed social issue, mentioned in tandem with marriage, is abortion. As a rule of thumb, those who are pro-abortion tend to favor so-called same-sex "marriage." Those who are pro-life are, most often, also supportive of historic, traditional, orthodox marriage between one man and one woman. What I find ironic is that those who are supposedly pro-choice in one area—abortion—suddenly become anti-choice in another area—homosexuality—claiming, "I cannot change; I was born this way." One might be born with a certain proclivity, but that does not equate to the need to act out that proclivity. One can struggle with same-sex attraction without having to participate in homosexual behavior.

ALL OF US WERE BORN *SOME* WAY

Each of us struggles with sin and each of us experiences different temptations. Struggling with sex and gender identities, whether it's gender-fluid, transgender, or homosexuality and same-sex attraction, is a manifestation of sin like struggling with lust, pornography, and adultery. We were born into a world of sin (1 John 2:16).

Allow me to give an illustration that almost every male will understand. Males have an inherent polyamorous proclivity. Polyamory is the capacity to be romantically involved with more than one person, in this case, more than one woman. I am not defending it, only explaining it. Consider these facts: husbands tend to have affairs more often than wives.[21] Men tend to be more addicted to pornography than women.[22] That is what I mean by the fact that males tend more toward polyamory, mistakenly thinking they can be involved with more than one woman at a time.

However, a male's inherent leaning towards certain desires is no excuse for him to act on it. We have a word for that—sin. My point is this: if the men want to do what is right, they simply do not yield to that instinct. So it is with all persons, including homosexuals. We are all *born a certain way*, with inclinations to do wrong things. But we can choose *not* to act on them. That is called maturity, self-restraint, and self-discipline. Likewise many are inclined to gluttony, lying, or thievery, but they do not have to yield to the temptation.

CHOICE OR COERCION

At the ESPYS, Caitlyn Jenner said, "Trans people deserve something vital; they deserve your respect."[23] Caitlyn Jenner's statement spoke to what the gay and transgender movement are truly after—approval, acceptance, and outright affirmation of their behavior. The radical LGBT cause demands this affirmation, even if that means infringing on others' freedom of thought, religion, and speech. They are not just looking for respect. They are demanding that everyone agree with their behavior choices.

On December 21, 2015, the New York City Commission on Human Rights expanded the city's Human Rights Laws to protect transgender and gender non-conforming individuals, those whose gender expression differs from traditional gender-based stereotypes. The protection under the new policy says that landlords, employers, and businesses will face civil penalties of fines up to $125,000 per violation and up to $250,000 "for violations that are the result of willful, wanton, or malicious conduct."[24] What is defined as malicious conduct?

- Intentionally refusing to use an individual's preferred title, name, or even pronoun.
- Refusing to allow an individual to use the single-sex facilities (bathrooms and locker rooms) or barring participation from single-sex programs of an individual's gender identity choice.
- Enforcing dress code standards that differ based on one's sex or gender.
- Refusing to provide healthcare benefits for employees that cover accommodations for individuals undergoing gender transition and gender-affirming care.[25]

Taking it a step further, the Obama administration has now demanded that the state of North Carolina repeal its "bathroom law." In addition, the administration has redefined Title IX and is demanding all universities bow to their transgender requirements. This is political correctness at its best, or should I say, its worst.

Over the years, I have had the privilege of meeting people who have become the victims of the radicalized Left, evidence that the real issue is not civil rights—which they already have—but coercion to affirm their lifestyle preferences. The following have faced threats, harassment, court costs, and excessive fines, all because they exercised their First Amendment rights:

- Barronelle Stutzman, owner of Arlene's Flowers, Richland, WA—although she readily sold flowers to homosexual customers, she could not, for religious reasons, use her artistic talent to glorify a same-sex "marriage" ceremony.[26]
- Blaine Adamson, owner of Hands-On Originals, Lexington, KY—for personal religious reasons, could not print a T-shirt for a gay pride parade celebrating homosexual behavior.[27]
- Elaine Huguenin, owner of Elane Photography, Albuquerque, NM—could not, as a matter of conscience, use her artistic talent to commemorate a same-sex commitment ceremony.[28]

This list could go on endlessly. I have a one-minute radio commentary called "The Garlow Perspective," which airs daily on 850 radio outlets. For two years, a major portion of my commentaries focused on legal cases all over the nation in which Christians were being fined or threatened with jail time for holding to biblical values regarding homosexuality and the definition of marriage.

This is not merely a U.S. phenomenon. A few years ago, I met and interviewed Pastor Ake Green from Borgholm, Sweden. He was sentenced to one month in prison for his view of homosexuality as sin, stemming from a sermon he preached to his church.[29] At a marriage conference in Paris, delegates from Africa told me that their continent is experiencing what they called "sexual colonization." They told me, "We were colonialized once" from the West, and now "we are being colonialized again" by the Obama administration, which is trying to force them to accept and affirm homosexual behavior.

Even our children cannot escape this debauchery and danger. Current SOGI (sexual orientation; gender identity) law battles are taking place in almost every state and most cities in America. This relentless coercion of perversity—men using the same bathrooms and locker room shower facilities as little girls—is not about having the same rights. It is about silencing—destroying anyone who dares oppose their moral depravity—and creating environments where our children and grandchildren are vulnerable.

For years the chant was, *what we do in our bedroom is our business.* If that is the case, then they should *keep* their business in their bedrooms.

THE BIBLE AND COMPLEMENTARITY

The Bible doesn't address Facebook's fifty-six alleged sex and gender identities. Why not? Because they do not exist. They are creations of someone's carnal imagination. However, the Bible does clearly provide us with biblical principles to be our guide.

Scripture supports the principle of God's intention of sexuality between men and women all throughout the Bible. The Bible does not discuss the issue of *being* a homosexual as an orientation (quite likely because there is no such thing. An orientation is a modern construct, something only taught in the past 150 years or so). The Bible does however speak about acts or actions. The act or practice of homosexual behavior is forbidden by Scripture.

There are six classic passages associated with homosexuality. In every case, homosexual practice is condemned. And what about the issue of same-sex "marriage"? There is not one passage affirming it. In contrast, both Genesis in the Old Testament (2:24) and Jesus in the New Testament (Matthew 19:4–6; Mark 10:6–9) affirm marriage as one man–one woman.

Let's do a quick review of the classic passages on homosexual behavior, and then list the imaginative revisionist attempts at casuistry—

the use of clever, but unsound reasoning to justify immoral behavior—that are used to thoroughly dispel the intent of the texts.

Genesis 19:4–8: "Before they had gone to bed, all the men from every part of the city of Sodom—both young and old—surrounded the house. They called to Lot, 'Where are the men who came to you tonight? Bring them out to us so that we can have sex with them.' Lot went outside to meet them and shut the door behind him and said, 'No, my friends. Don't do this wicked thing.... don't do anything to these men....'"

This is the well-known account of Sodom and Gomorrah. The pro-homosexual revisionists rewrite the story to make the sin not homosexual behavior, but inhospitality.[30] According to them, the fact that these were homosexuals desiring to have sex with men is of no consequence. The real problem, they claim, is gang rape. Further, they cite Ezekiel 16:49 as proof that the problem is not homosexuality.

But the very next verse (Ezekiel 16:50) describes Sodom's sin as "abomination"—the same word used in Leviticus 18:22 to describe homosexual sins. In addition, Jude 7 talks explicitly about the "sexual immorality and perversion" of Sodom and Gomorrah. Contrary to pro-homosexual eisegesis—reading into the biblical text what they want it to say—the text condemns the practice of homosexuality.

Leviticus 18:22: "Do not lie with a man as one lies with a woman; that is detestable."

Leviticus 20:13: "If a man lies with a man as one lies with a woman, both of them have done what is detestable. They must be put to death; their blood will be on their own heads."

These verses seem clear. Yet those wanting to justify immoral behavior contend that the Old Testament also prohibits other actions—such as eating pork and shellfish, wearing clothes with mixed fiber or mixing seeds—yet we don't follow *those* prohibitions. But ceremonial laws or symbolic laws were temporary by design; in contrast, the moral laws continue to apply today. The prohibition for mixing of clothing fibers and seeds was a command unique to the Jews of that time to keep them separate from pagans who did these things for religious, mystical, or magical purposes. The command regarding what to eat and not eat was unique to that time and did not carry over into the New Testament, because the cultural landscape had changed.

However, *the prohibition against the practice of homosexual behavior continued into the New Testament and has been affirmed by every scholar and church leader for the past two thousand years.*

Romans 1:26–27: "Even their women exchanged natural sexual relations for unnatural ones; in the same way, men committed shameful acts with other men and received in themselves the due penalty for their error."

How do those that practice homosexual behavior get around this one? The logic gets more complicated. Surely, they claim, Paul could not be writing about loving, same-sex relations. So they engineer the notion that Paul is speaking of men and young boys in sexual relations. Or others contend that Paul was talking about ancient pagan temple practices.

1 Corinthians 6:9–11: Do you not know that the wicked will not inherit the kingdom of God? Do not be deceived: Neither the sexually immoral nor idolaters nor adulterers nor male prostitutes nor homosexual offenders nor thieves nor the greedy nor drunkards nor slanderers nor swindlers will inherit the kingdom of God. And that is what some of you were. But you were washed, you were sanctified, you were justified in the name of the Lord Jesus Christ and by the Spirit of our God.

1 Timothy 1:10: "...and immoral men and homosexuals and kidnappers and liars and perjurers, and whatever else is contrary to sound teaching."

These two passages are quite clear, are they not? Not to those who want to justify ungodly behavior. One hermeneutical (the science of interpretation) principle is to take language at face value. Another principle is that when you come to a difficult verse, allow the rest of the Bible to help you interpret it.

One would think that when Genesis says we are made male and female and those two are to come together as one in covenantal marriage, that truth would be the end of any argument to defend the practice of homosexual behavior. Or if one simply used Natural Law (that is, reasoning and nature, not the Bible) one observes that the male anatomy and the female anatomy fit together. In addition, the procreation of the human race depends upon a sperm and an egg uniting, thus male-female pairing.

When building a house, every plumber knows he must join the male and female ends of pipes. Every electrician knows he must join the male and female ends of cords and sockets. What could possibly be so difficult to understanding that male-male connections violate Natural Law, as do female-female connections? In the 1 Corinthians and 1 Timothy verses above, those who promote homosexual behavior explain away the term homosexual to mean simply "dirty old men." Or they say that Paul just did not understand loving, monogamous, homosexual relationships, therefore he is just—well—wrong.

The bottom line: attempts to explain away all the texts dealing with homosexuality fail.

THE BIBLE AND TRANSGENDER

Attempts to biblically justify *trans* lifestyles fail as well. Deuteronomy 22:5 is quite blunt: "A woman must not wear men's clothing, nor a man wear women's clothing, for the Lord your God detests anyone who does this."

God did not make mistakes as He created men and women. Psalms 139:13–14 describes the creation process, "For you created my inmost being; you knit me together in my mother's womb. I praise you because I am fearfully and wonderfully made; your works are wonderful; I know that full well."

God gave each of us a gender from the time we were knit together in our mother's womb. Every time our culture approves transgender, transsexual, and gender-fluidity, it diminishes God and His creation. It communicates a message that God sometimes makes gender mistakes, and instead of His creation living as He designed—both male and female—we attempt to re-create ourselves. We must ask ourselves, who is our God? Who is the Creator? Is He the Lord of the Universe, or are we?

HOW ARE WE TO RESPOND?

Having said all the above, we—as followers of Jesus—desire to be redemptive in a very wounded, broken world. Those struggling with sexual identity need our compassionate love. Their lot in life is not enhanced by us coddling them in their sin, but by loving them enough to explain the spectacular truth of the Gospel, the steps to forgiveness, the pathway to healing, and the empowerment of the Holy Spirit. True biblical compassion calls for us to pray and fast for those who struggle to be set free from any of the demons within them, just as people stood with us so that we could be free from the sins in our lives.

Jesus came "full of grace and truth" (John 1:14). We must do the same. I have a tendency to want to reverse the order: truth and grace. I would rather come in truth first, and grace later. Jesus came in grace first, and truth later. May we do the same.

Second, we are to respond in love to anyone struggling with sex and gender identity. Having a temptation is not sin. Acting on it is. It is imperative to reach out to all in the spirit of love. We do not have to capitulate on this issue as so many do in the present day. We can unabashedly label sin as sin. But neither must we become hateful. We can remain loving and respectful of all.

The greatest commandment has not changed. It is still to love. At the same time, we are to boldly speak the truth to them in love. Love does not mean to be silent. The greatest love is spoken with truth and compassion—sometimes that means it is tough love. "And now these three remain: faith, hope and love. But the greatest of these is love" (1 Corinthians 13:13).

We must stand with Jesus who said, "For this reason" (Matthew 19:5). For what reason? The fact that we were made as either male or female. The proper sexual relationship between the two (and there are only two) genders is within the institution God has created for the good of all mankind, namely marriage.

But I must close with great news! Did you notice in 1 Corinthians 6:11 the glorious truth that people can be forgiven and set free? *"And that is what some of you were.* But you were washed, you were sanctified, you were justified in the name of the Lord Jesus Christ and by the Spirit of our God." That is the spectacular truth that applies to us all, since all of us are, in fact, sinners. This passage answers the nagging question, *can someone involved in homosexuality, and all the other sins that Paul mentions* (for example 1 Timothy 1:8–11; Colossians 3:5, 8; Galatians 5:19–21), *be forgiven and healed?* Yes. A resounding yes!

But allow me to illustrate how the healing may vary. Two alcoholics may have different outcomes—one may never desire another drink, while the other one struggles the rest of his life. I cannot explain why one has more struggles than the other. But both *can* walk sober and clean. So it is with the sexually addicted, be it adulterers, fornicators, those addicted to pornography, those who lust, those who engage in homosexual behavior, and all the other sins listed above. All can come to a point of forgiveness through what Christ did on the cross and the empowerment that comes from the indwelling of the Holy Spirit.

CHAPTER TWELVE

HEALTHCARE

*The mania for giving the Government power to meddle
with the private affairs of cities or citizens is likely to cause
endless trouble.*[1]

—MARK TWAIN

was stunned when the attorney called and informed me that our church insurance was now covering elective abortions. "But we would *never* pay for *abortions*!"

"Well, sorry to inform you, but you *are* covering abortions," he replied.

Unbeknownst to us, on August 22, 2014, an unelected bureaucrat in Sacramento, California, had arbitrarily decided that every single insurance provider would have to pay for the killing of unborn babies.[2] A governmental fiat—to kill babies!—forced on us all. Period.

We were not informed; not by the state, not by our insurance company. A very smart attorney found out about it and informed me.

How is healthcare coercion of churches and others to pay for abortions possible? That is not health*care*. That is health *destruction*.

YOU OR THE GOVERNMENT?

Who is responsible for your health? You, if you are of age. If you're unable to care for yourself, then the family unit is responsible. And if no familial help is available, the responsibility falls to the Church. If the Church fails, it passes the responsibility on to the community-at-large. If the community does not look after the individual, *then* it falls to the government. But our nation tragically starts with the government. Our government then takes citizens' earnings by coercion and reallocates funds to those who need them, all because you and I did not take responsibility for the destitute.

Matthew 25:36 (NASB) states, "Naked, and you clothed Me; I was sick, and you visited Me; I was in prison, and you came to Me." He's not addressing the government. He's talking to the people of God.

We have a healthcare system in obvious need of reform. Pharmaceutical and medical costs are astronomically high, and faulty insurance leaves many in desperate situations trying to support their loved ones. So government sought to find a solution. In 2010, President Obama signed into law the Patient Protection and Affordable Care Act, better known as Obamacare. The hope of the new law was to expand patient coverage, control healthcare costs, and improve healthcare delivery. But by stepping outside of governmental jurisdiction, this measure has been far from successful.

Obamacare forces compliance. It is not an optional program; it is mandatory. The law now requires everyone to purchase health insurance. Don't comply, and you will be faced with a fine each month—either 2.5 percent of your household income or $695 per adult and $347 per child living in your house, whichever is *higher*. The fee is called the individual responsibility payment: everyone must pay his or her fair share.[3] Take a look at what has happened since the Affordable Care Act.

RELIGIOUS LIBERTY AND DEATH PANELS

A group of Catholic nuns called the Little Sisters of the Poor runs over thirty nursing homes around the country. Today, they are forced to obtain contraception, sterilization, and abortion coverage for their employees through a third-party insurer, despite the fact this violates their religious beliefs.[4] Dozens of non-profit and for-profit groups have filed lawsuits against the government over this issue of contraception coverage. Some, like Hobby Lobby, took the issue all the way to the Supreme Court.[5]

All these groups claim the Affordable Care Act violates the Religious Freedom Restoration Act (RFRA). However, the Obama administration created a loophole to avoid religious pushback. A religious exception form can be submitted, and, if approved, the government will require a third party to provide sterilization, contraceptives, and abortions. However, *the costs would still be funded by the original company.*[6] Did the Obama administration actually think Bible-believing Christians would fall for this deception?

The Church, for the most part, opposed abortion when it became legal in 1973, but because it was a choice outside of their control many stayed silent. Today the Church is not only forced to acknowledge abortion's legality, it must watch federal revenue support abortion-providers such as Planned Parenthood and 58 million mothers[7] choose to kill their babies. Now it is forced to directly and openly participate in abortion via health insurance coverage. As I stated earlier, our church was one of those who has now—thanks to the Department of Managed Healthcare of the State of California—been forced to pay for abortions. When the freedom of choice is taken away, infringement on religious liberty soon follows.

It gets worse. The Affordable Care Act, Obamacare, set in place a board that would recommend savings to the Medicare program. The board, the Independent Payment Advisory Board (IPAB), is made up of fifteen *unelected* appointed bureaucrats.[8] The panel helps decide where costs could be cut and when and what kind of care patients receive.

Speaker of the House Paul Ryan says of this panel, "This unelected panel exists only to take control away from patients and ration care—and it's seniors who will suffer the consequences."[9] Some called this unelected decision-making group between the patient and doctor relationship a "death panel." Decisions regarding medical care have been taken from the individual and are now made by the government. In many cases a government panel will ultimately decide what treatment is best and what constitutes a reasonable quality of life—with the goal to lower costs to the absolute minimum. Think about it: when the bottom line is minimizing costs, when would a worthy but costly life ever trump a cost-effective, expedited death?

WHAT IS THE ROLE OF GOVERNMENT IN HEALTHCARE?

There are nineteen enumerated federal powers found in the Constitution; healthcare is not one of them. Coercion from the government, at any level, to purchase health insurance is outside the scope of the government's core biblical mandate to "protect the citizenry by punishing evil" (Romans 13:4; 1 Peter 2:14). The issue at stake is one of coercion, assuming authority beyond the bounds of government's rightful jurisdiction. This path leads not towards individual freedom, but instead to ungodly socialism.

One only has to look around the world to see the overwhelming evidence that the private sector will always outperform the government:

- Consider the DMV (Department of Motor Vehicles) and how ineffectively it is run. Why? No competition.
- The U.S. Post Office is no longer the best and fastest way to deliver packages. Why? Because we have other competitive choices available to us.
- Government-run healthcare for our veterans has resulted in hundreds of examples of poor care and lack of treatment. Why? Because veterans are a captive audience with very few alternatives.
- Public utilities costs continue to rise even though we conserve more and more. Why? Because we have little recourse to turn elsewhere.

The private sector performs tasks quicker, easier, better, and more thoroughly than any bureaucracy because there is no monopoly. In the private sector, the customer encourages healthy competition by purchasing products or services from the company that best fits their needs. Companies, unlike the government, are forced to listen to what the public wants and continually adapt and innovate. If they don't, they eventually disappear and are replaced by those that better provide what is needed.

There are two issues at the root of the healthcare problem and biblical solutions that would solve both. Dale Bellis, Executive Director of Liberty HealthShare, has broken down two core flaws and their simple biblical solutions: cost and access to treatment.

COST

Obamacare promised lower costs, remember? How did that work out? In all but one state, the costs have risen. In Minnesota, costs have spiked over 47 percent.[10]

Healthcare costs skyrocketed because we have a third-party system; someone else is paying the bills. The culprits are the insurance companies, the government, and the employer healthcare plans. When someone else is paying the bills, more often than not, the patient does not know about nor care about the actual cost. For example, after a hospital stay, we usually don't even see the bill because we didn't pay for it. This system breeds a sense of entitlement, because ultimately someone else is responsible for footing the bill. Americans aren't paying directly out of pocket and the resulting apathy allows costs to rise.

The solution is personal healthcare responsibility. If every American were responsible for his or her own healthcare costs, the system would transform overnight. Patients would want to avoid unnecessary costs and would naturally allow the free-market system of negotiation and competition to drive prices down. When individuals operate in a self-paid system, they have freedom and liberty and the motivation to control their own care.

There are times when the cost exceeds what an individual can pay. Christian medical sharing companies have risen to meet these needs. Thousands of Christians have committed to meet one another's needs and share the healthcare expenses on a fair basis. This system has been working phenomenally well for many. There are currently four main medical sharing ministries in the United States:

- Christian Healthcare Ministries
- Medi-Share
- Samaritan Ministries
- Liberty HealthShare

These companies are living out Galatians 6:10: "Therefore, as we have opportunity, let us do good to all people, especially to those who belong to the family of believers" and Galatians 6:2 (ESV): "Bear one another's burdens, and so fulfill the law of Christ," as well as Acts 2:44–45 (ESV), "All who believed were together and held everything in common, and they were selling their possessions and belongings and distributing the proceeds to all, as any had need." This is the biblical principle that is found in medical ministry sharing—where Christians come together voluntarily to bear the burdens of one another.

If you're wondering if this can be done—it already has been done. Christian Healthcare Ministries was one of the first to lead the way. And for nearly thirty-five years, they have shared more than $1 billion in medical bills and served over one hundred thousand people. CEO of Medi-Share, Tony Meggs, said, "A healthcare crisis will always be a test of faith. We place faith in the wisdom of doctors and the hands of surgeons. This growing number of Christians across America are placing less faith in insurance companies and more faith in the prayers and support of like-minded Christians."[11]

Just like the church of Acts, Christians are both caring for one another and wisely planning for the future.

LIMITED ACCESS TO MEDICAL DOCTORS

The healthcare system is currently set up so that you see your doctor when you are sick. This is flawed for a few reasons. First, doctors are inundated with sick patients. Researchers are predicting we will have a shortage of ninety thousand doctors by 2025.[12] And with the continued governmental intrusion into our private health issues, doctors are leaving the medical field. Imagine being told one day that there is no doctor.

Second, doctors are financially motivated to only see you when you are sick. The doctor is incentivized for every sick visit you make and every prescription he writes. This is the way the economic engine works. This is a *sick care* system not a *healthcare* system. Consequently, doctors are forced to spend time reacting to people's illnesses, instead of spending the needed time to get to the core of the problems.

Because of these incentives, a doctor spends seven minutes on average with each patient—hardly enough time to dig deep into health problems. There has to be a change in this model.

The solution is a biblical healthcare model where your body is not your own (1 Corinthians 6:19). We have a spiritual obligation to care for our bodies—the temple of the Holy Spirit. 1 Corinthians 10:31 says, "So, whether you eat or drink, or whatever you do, do all for the glory of God." Clearly, being irresponsible with our own health will contribute to the impractical condition of our healthcare system as it creates an overload of sick patients for doctors to manage. Preventive care is consistent with what John wrote in 3 John 1:2 when he said, "Beloved, I pray that all may go well with you and that you may be in good health, as it goes well with your soul." John made the astute observation that a well soul leads to a well body. Taking care of our spiritual needs allows us to better understand our spiritual responsibility to care for the bodies that God has given to us that we may serve Him more fully and honor what He has entrusted to our care. Our bodies belong to Him!

Liberty HealthShare is one company that has sought to solve the practical issues of access and personal health responsibility with a subscription-based doctor model. Instead of individuals paying access fees to see their doctors when they are sick, they pay a monthly family doctor fee. This allows them to visit their doctor as often as needed and provides the doctor with an added incentive to keep them well so that they see the patient less. Instead of being your sick-care only doctor, he or she becomes your life-coach, committed to being pro-active about your health alongside you. This model incentivizes the doctor to think about your healthcare preventatively, not simply to prescribe a pill for your symptoms in a seven-minute scrutiny.

Liberty HealthShare members now have direct access to their primary care physicians. Doctors enjoy this model as well because instead of having to see thousands of patients—they instead care for four hundred to six hundred families on a per-year subscription basis.

Bureaucracy disappears as doctors spend less time on insurance paperwork and more time with their patients. Medical practices all over the country are beginning to switch from the point-of-service model to direct primary care.

Access also increases when medical providers utilize technology. Liberty HealthShare and a company called Video Medicine are leading the way with newfound doctor access through a video call. Eighty percent of diagnoses can be given via a simple conversation between a physician and patient, saving both parties time and expenses.

A BIBLICAL WORLDVIEW

Solutions exist that are consistent with a biblical understanding of bodily stewardship, and that include doctors trained to help holistically without red tape or bureaucracy. These solutions to our nation's current healthcare problems aren't only for Christians; these biblical principles and truths can help solve the national healthcare crisis for everyone.

Be encouraged. We don't have to wait for the government or new politicians to solve this issue. The body of Christ can do it today by living out the Word of God.

PART IV

ECONOMICS

CHAPTER THIRTEEN

CAPITALISM AND SOCIALISM

The first lesson of economics is scarcity: there is never enough of anything to fully satisfy all those who want it. The first lesson of politics is to disregard the first lesson of economics.[1]

—THOMAS SOWELL

I s capitalism a dirty word? What is it? Why was capitalism once considered a good thing in America? What happened to cause so many to view it negatively?

The Merriam-Webster Dictionary defines capitalism as, "an economic system characterized by private or corporate ownership of capital goods, by investments that are determined by private decision, and by prices, production, and the distribution of goods that are determined mainly by competition in a free market." But a cleaner way to say this is that capitalism is an economic system where a person can freely offer something for sale to a willing buyer at an agreed price.

For capitalism to function, a nation needs to have economic liberty to acquire wealth through honest work, religious liberty to instill God-honoring values throughout the culture, and political liberty from self-serving political oppression. When all these factors exist, economic growth and widespread prosperity occur. Historically, Adam Smith, the Scottish philosopher and pioneer of political economy, described this condition of mutual benefit as the workings of an "invisible hand" that allows people to serve their own interest, while bringing positive economic results for others.[2]

IS CAPITALISM BIBLICAL?

Yes, and no. The word is not found in the Bible, but the moral underpinnings of capitalism definitely are. Even though God cursed the ground after Adam's fall in the Garden of Eden (Genesis 3:17–19), God didn't make hard work a curse. In fact, work—caring for the Garden—pre-dated the entrance of sin. Work is God-honoring and part of our reflecting the image of God, who also works. As Jesus so clearly said, "My Father has been working until now and I have been working…" (John 5:17, NKJV).

Biblically, God expects productivity (fruit) from mankind as we work and till his creation (Genesis 2:15; 9:1). The obvious reason for our hard work is to be able to enjoy the benefits of our labor, as it both provides for our families and honors the Lord at the same time.

Enjoying the fruit of our labor is also encapsulated in our Declaration of Independence in the words "life, liberty and the pursuit of happiness."[3] The phase "pursuit of happiness" has been the subject of hot debate. In the 1600s, British philosopher John Locke wrote that the role of government is to secure "life, liberty and property," with no mention of happiness.[4] Thomas Jefferson listed life and liberty, but not property. "Pursuit of happiness" might have been borrowed from Samuel Johnson or from other writings by John Locke.

The question is, what does it mean? One understanding is, in part, the ability to acquire and own property. It encompasses the rights of employers and employees to work for their own benefit. It includes investing in someone else's enterprise and accumulating savings from one's surplus to protect against an uncertain future.

But intrinsic to an economic construct like capitalism is an acceptable moral framework to govern personal actions and decisions. Without a biblically moral base to guide and restrain human nature, any economic system (just like any human activity) will crumble. Remember the words of Jeremiah the prophet when he said, "The heart is deceitful above all things, and desperately sick, who can understand?" (Jeremiah 17:9, NASB).

CRONY CAPITALISM

Obviously, I am not advocating unfettered capitalism. Just like any good thing, it can be abused. *Crony capitalism* or *cronyism* is the appointment of family, friends and close associations without proper vetting of their qualifications. Not surprisingly, crony capitalism most often applies to close business associates of governmental figures, who receive favored status in government contracts, grants, regulations or taxes, based solely on the friendship. This is theft.

The capitalism I am advocating is one outlined by Judeo-Christian values, such as honesty, forthrightness, integrity, and openness. Utilitarianism—whatever seems best for the most—or some hyperpragmatic form of capitalism is inherently anti-biblical. But the desire to work hard and gain from one's labors is good, right, biblical, and God-honoring.

There are no perfect economic systems in a fallen world, but history shows that of all systems, capitalism has done more to improve the economic plight of the world than any other approach.[5] This really shouldn't be surprising. The biblical model allows people to work hard while recognizing a moral obligation to use the fruit of one's labor to generously help those who are truly needy. Reverend John Wesley said it well: "Gain all you can, save all you can, and give all you can."[6] In three words: compassionate Christian capitalism.

IS CAPITALISM SELFISH?

Capitalism itself isn't selfish, but the heart behind it can be. A system is not inherently selfish; people are. People can be wealthy and greedy, or poor and greedy. Greediness doesn't depend on economic status. In fact, my observation of life tells me that there are as many greedy people who are poor as there are those who own billions. If one person has a lot of money and another person is demanding the rich man's money, which one is greedy? I would contend that it is the person who wants what others have.

The Occupy Wall Street movement had as many greedy, covetous persons as the number of Wall Street bankers they were assailing. Show me a person who uses their welfare dollars to buy lottery tickets and play the casino slots, and you will see as much greed as an inner city slumlord. Greed and covetousness are not defined by capitalism. Socialism, as well, is neither inherently greedy nor covetous. But the people advocating socialism often are. They want that which they have not earned. Every child—if well taught—knows that is called selfishness.

For the record, most people become wealthy by serving. Bill Gates and Steve Jobs served America well. As we write, I am using products developed by the companies founded by these two billionaires. I am so thankful for the computer and cell phone products they created. My life is better for it. And for the record, though I am not a wealthy man, I have never resented the fact that they were both immensely wealthy. Remember how they got the wealth: serving us. We liked what they made. We bought their goods and services.

Furthermore, nowhere in Scripture are riches condemned as evil. This shouldn't be surprising since the Lord owns it all, including the cattle on a thousand hills (Psalms 50:10). What God condemns is the ungodly use of riches or the ungodly *love* of money (1 Timothy 6:10), not money itself. Some of the heroes of our faith were very wealthy: Job, Abraham, Isaac, and Jacob. Wealthy believers in the New Testament were generous in the support of the Gospel, including Lydia and Aquila and Priscilla. They are never condemned for their wealth, but knew to be generous to others as God had been generous to them.

There are also examples of rich men that were judged severely for their wicked selfishness. Nabal's refusal to assist David in 1 Samuel 25 is a classic case of rejecting a clear request for help. In the New Testament, Jesus confronted a rich young ruler about his greater love of possessions than for any concern about the poor (Matthew 19:16–22).

Free people who work in free markets have the incentive to work hard and take risks because they get to keep the fruit of their labors. We need successful entrepreneurs to invent products and create businesses that provide desirable goods and services. This creates jobs and income for others. Clearly, God calls us to be good stewards of our unique gifts, talents and opportunities. We are to glorify Him with hard work knowing "the worker deserves his wages" (1 Timothy 5:18), but also that "the one who is unwilling to work shall not eat" (2 Thessalonians 3:10). Admittedly some cannot work; they are incapacitated. Knowing which category someone falls into requires wisdom, backed by a heart tender to the plight of the legitimately poor and those that have been unjustly impoverished by the sinful actions of others.

IS SOCIALISM A MORE EQUITABLE FORM OF CAPITALISM?

Quite likely the most shocking, naive and benighted statement ever uttered on economics by a sitting U.S. president was made by

President Obama in March 2016. He told Argentinian youth that there is little difference between communism or socialism and capitalism, so they should just "choose from what works."[7] Contradicting himself immediately, he acknowledged that Havana, Cuba, a city in a socialist state he had recently visited, had made little progress since the 1950s, and that the incentives of a market-based economy were superior.[8]

Let us be clear: the differences between capitalism and socialism are enormous. They are essentially polar opposites. Globally, socialism is the only other major, rival economic system to its own sister communism and to capitalism. Some people say that the difference between socialism and communism is that a communist is a socialist with a gun.

Karl Marx, the German philosopher and the intellectual fountainhead of socialism, argued that religion was "the opiate of the people"[9] and made people numb to the economic inequalities of this world due to a fixation on the next life. But he was wrong. His systems have produced massive human suffering and death—on a scale previously unknown to the world.

The solution to mankind's problems as proposed by socialism was simple: "From each according to their ability and to each according to their need."[10] There's no need for private property; we'll share everything equally. To ensure equitable arrangements, an allegedly benevolent state would own and apportion everything. No one should work for selfish interest, rather everyone must work for society's greater good.

What could be more reasonable or fair? That's the catch. Socialism looks good on paper, but it is contrary to the way human nature works in a fallen world. Show me any group of people in which—after their labors—they all receive the same amount, and eventually they will all begin doing as little as they possibly can. Incentive disappears. Paul wrote to young Timothy that "the worker deserves his wages" (1 Timothy 5:18). He also valued work so greatly that he declared, as noted earlier, "the one who is unwilling to work shall not eat" (2 Thessalonians 3:10).

Socialism punishes the successful and forces them to give up the fruit of their labor to others who have elected to play it safe or simply exploit the system. Socialism punishes entrepreneurship while rewarding mediocrity. Incentive, risk, and creativity wither, and economic stagnation and collapse soon follow. Eventually, a socialist system will devolve into a vicious, totalitarian empire that cannot sustain itself. Winston Churchill aptly defined socialism as "a philosophy of failure, the creed of ignorance, and the gospel of envy,"[11] and "its inherent value is the equal sharing of misery."[12]

IS SOCIALISM BIBLICAL?

Some have tried to argue the Bible supports socialism. They appeal to Acts 2:45, which says, "And they were selling their possessions and belongings and distributing the proceeds to all, as any had need." But remember the historical context. This was right after the Day of Pentecost when some 3,000 religious pilgrims from all over the world were visiting Jerusalem and came to believe the Gospel.

Up to this point, only about 120 people constituted the core of Christian believers. Now, they suddenly had to take on the spiritual and physical responsibility for the 3,000 who had just embraced Jesus as the Messiah. It would not be good for them to return home; the new believers needed to stay and be discipled in the faith.

The 120 gladly sacrificed to provide the needed hospitality. To do so, they sold their possessions to make ends meet. Note carefully, this behavior was not coerced by the government; it was not spreading the wealth by redistribution. This was *voluntary* charity between believers. In fact, it was a perfect illustration of what Paul encouraged believers in Corinth to be: generous to one another (2 Corinthians 8 and 9).

There are many biblical passages on caring for the poor. But the need is never met by the coercive arm of the socialistic state taking one's property and giving it to another. It is met by the "poor tax" collected (Deuteronomy 14:28) for religious leaders—administered locally—and by caring landowners, leaving fallen grapes (Leviticus 19:10) and the corners of the fields (Leviticus 23:22) to be harvested by those who lacked. Care for the poor is so close to the heart of God that He placed the role with the people of God. Apparently, He knew the government could not handle it properly.

Any forced redistribution of the fruit of a man's labor violates God's command not to steal. Theft is still theft, even when it's the government picking your pocket. Whether by a gun (a thief) or through a tax (by the IRS), the impact is still the same: you no longer have what you earned.

AMERICA NEEDS BIBLICAL CORRECTION

Our nation follows a largely capitalist system that has been undermined by socialistic welfare programs. After decades of our War on Poverty, we are approaching $20 trillion in debt[13] and on the brink of national bankruptcy.

In addition, government has actually helped create crony capitalism by massively interfering in the free market. Government does not have any biblical role in picking winners and losers by unfairly granting government contracts, manipulating laws and regulations, or by bailing out failing businesses. This process undermines the natural checks and balances within the free market that keep an economy healthy.

May God grant us, as Americans, an opportunity for a distinctly Judeo-Christian framework of capitalism and a government that will follow its constitutional limitations and allow citizens to be free to create in the image of God.

CHAPTER FOURTEEN

TAXES

The difference between death and taxes is death doesn't get worse every time Congress meets.[1]

—WILL ROGERS

For a nation to try to tax itself into prosperity is like a man standing in a bucket and trying to lift himself up by the handle.[2]

—WINSTON CHURCHILL

Collecting more taxes than absolutely necessary is legalized robbery.[3]

—CALVIN COOLIDGE

When the government becomes irresponsible in exercising its power to tax, all personal freedoms are at risk, including our duty to adequately provide for ourselves, our family, those who are less fortunate.[4]

Ask any believer about taxation in the Bible, and he or she will likely quote, "Give to Caesar what is Caesar's, and to God what is God's." A superficial glance at the text might conclude that Jesus is saying, *Pay your taxes to the government, and then go and worship God.* But his meaning is considerably deeper and more profound. Jesus' response came as a result of a question asked of him by his critics in Matthew 22:17–22, attempting to entrap him: "Is it right to pay taxes to Caesar or not?" Jesus could have simply said *yes*, but he didn't. Why not?

In the ancient Roman Empire, Caesar was worshipped as a god. The failure to say "Caesar is Lord" cost Polycarp his life.[5] The cult of emperor worship was widespread, and failure to comply was costly.[6] In this text Jesus responded to a question with a question. He asked, "'Whose portrait is this? And whose inscription?' and they replied, 'Caesar's,'"(Matthew 22:20–21).

But his response, "Give to Caesar what is Caesar's, and to God what is God's" did not actually address their question regarding taxes. If so, the text would not have said they were amazed and "left him and went away," for what is so amazing about giving an answer that equates to, *Sure, pay your taxes*. Surely that would not amaze them. But Jesus took them to a different level with his response.

In effect, he said, "Either Caesar is Lord, or God is Lord. So stop giving to Caesar that which isn't his. Stop your idolatry." Later, Christians, refusing to say "Caesar is Lord," would develop the first of all creeds, simply, "Jesus is Lord." This verse addresses the issue of ultimate allegiance. If Caesar is Lord, then God isn't. *That* is what amazed them. *That* is why they retreated. They could have responded to his answer if it simply meant to pay your taxes. But it didn't simply mean that. True to Jesus' normal *modus operandi*, his answer cut much deeper.

However, Romans 13 *does* address taxes. Paul stated, "For because of this [the role of government to punish evil and reward good] you also pay taxes, for the authorities are ministers of God, attending to this very thing. Pay to all what is owed to them: taxes to whom taxes are owed, revenue to whom revenue is owed, respect to whom respect is owed, honor to whom honor is owed" (Romans 13:6–7, ESV). Obviously, taxes are not evil, as such, just as money is not evil—only the love of it (1 Timothy 6:10). At face value, Scripture supports the notion of taxation. And God is not an anarchist. Thus, he commands us to support civil government because civil governance is intended for our good and requires funding. But how much? Is there a legitimate amount a government can tax? Or, better yet, are there limits to how much tax we should be forced to pay?

CURRENT TAX PLANS

In general terms, here are the current tax plans that are being used or are being proposed:

- **Progressive tax:** Based on income: This is what is currently used. The higher your income level, the higher your tax becomes. Some people like it because it makes people with more income pay more—not merely the same percentage—but a higher percentage with each higher level of income. Some people don't like it because it treats people differently, even unfairly.
- **Fair tax:** Based on what is purchased: This would be a consumption tax. You would pay a percentage of tax— say 30 percent—based on what you buy, excluding certain necessities. Some people like it because all income and payroll taxes are gone. It allows greater privacy. Some people are uncertain, because it is new and untested, and it shifts tax collection from the IRS to businesses.
- **Flat tax:** Constant percentage of income: Everyone has the same rate or same percentage—period. Some people like it because it is consistent for everyone and simple. Gone are the long, complex tax forms. Some people don't like it because someone that is at the poverty level would pay the same percentage as a billionaire.[7]

Of course, the above descriptions are oversimplifications, but our purpose here is not to give detailed taxation plans. Our concern is to ask: are certain tax plans, in principle, distinctively biblical or unbiblical?

A BIBLICAL TAX CODE

But what is a biblical tax? Is it like a tithe, that is, 10 percent? My wife and I attended the August 6, 2015, GOP presidential debate held in Cleveland, OH, in which then-candidate Dr. Ben Carson said that the tax should be 10 percent, "based on tithing, because I think God is a pretty fair guy."[8]

Is that true? Should the government only get what God gets in the tithe? If so, the revenues to government would be vastly reduced—which might not be all bad.

Currently, tax rates can go as high as 39.6 percent.[9] There were primarily two types of taxes in the Old Testament:

- A **poll tax**, also called head tax, meaning a set amount per person (Exodus 30:11–16). Every male above the age of twenty paid the same amount. It had to be low enough so that a poor person could afford it. Exodus 30:15 stated that "the rich shall not give more, and the poor shall not give less." The genius of this low but universal tax is that everyone participated. Contrast that with America, in which nearly 50 percent of citizens pay no income taxes. In ancient Israel, even the poorest had the dignified role of helping to carry the load, even if the amount was small.
- The **tithe**, or 10 percent, was "holy unto the Lord" (Leviticus 27:32; 1 Samuel 8:15, 17), to carry on religious function.[10]

PROPERTY TAX

One might ask, *what about property tax?* In the Bible, there is neither land tax nor property tax. The short answer for this is that "the earth is the Lord's, and the fullness thereof" (Exodus 9:29; Deuteronomy 10:14; Psalms 24:1; 1 Corinthians 10:26). People were taxed on their productivity—what they had produced with labor—but did not pay a tax on land. It wasn't ultimately theirs. It was God's. The tax on productivity was a flat tax of 10 percent.

FEUDAL OR ALLODIAL

The absence of a property tax raises the issue of how we own property. Let's suppose you bought a house. You own it, right? Not quite. If you fail to make your monthly payments, you will discover that the mortgage company owns it. But suppose that you pay off the mortgage and owe nothing. The house is finally yours, correct? No. You don't really own it.

If you fail to continue paying an annual, assessed fee by the state or county government, they will take your house. The house might be worth $1 million. You may only owe $100 in taxes. They will still take your house. Why? Because you own your house *feudally*, a word that comes from the feudal system. Failing to pay the government annually means you have, in a way, only a tenancy of your house, in contrast to *allodial* ownership, which is totally free and clear of *any* government claims.

CONSUMPTION TAX

There's no obvious example nor biblical justification for a consumption tax (fair tax). The entire pattern of taxation and tithing is focused on what one produces—whether based on wages paid for one's labor, or the first fruit of what one produces from the land. In fact, the first fruit of the increase from our work belongs to the Lord (Proverbs 3:9–10). This payment is an acknowledgement of God's mercy and provision and bountifully providing for our needs. The reverse side of this—taxing or tithing on what is received (or consumed)—would seem to disproportionately impact those who struggle to provide for themselves and does not seem to be in keeping with God's pattern of provision.

Does this mean a consumption tax is not allowed biblically? Romans 13:6–7 lays out taxes and revenue to be paid to whom they are owed: the civil authorities that God has placed over the people for their well-being. There is not a lot of specificity as to what type of taxes are meant in these verses, but it is clear that Rome levied all kinds of different taxes to support the needs of its growing empire. It seems reasonable, therefore, to acknowledge the government's freedom to levy any number of different taxes as long as they don't violate a clear prohibition from Scripture.

THE POWER TO TAX

The power to tax can be a lethal proposition. Chief Justice John Marshall, handing down one of the most basic decisions of U.S. constitutional law in the 1819 Supreme Court case of *McCulloch v. Maryland*, stated that "the power to tax involves the power to destroy."[11]

Let's go back to our original pursuit in this chapter. What are the biblical responsibilities for government? At the same time, what does the Constitution stipulate? At the moment, military and welfare comprise most of the government's budget.

As noted in our chapter on the roles of government, the federal government is charged with protecting the citizenry with national defense. A church is not. It can be argued that in light of Romans 13:4; 1 Timothy 2:2; and 1 Peter 2:14 the responsibility of government includes wielding the sword to maintain order, punish the evildoer and protect its citizens, something that requires a consistent and well-resourced presence of military or militia power. National military preparedness is a legitimate, biblically defensible, portion of our government's budget.

Unlike national defense (which is the role of the state), isn't the issue of the poor a job for the Church (synagogues, faith communities) to handle? We have become so accustomed to the state handling welfare issues that probably few have ever considered the possibility that there might be another way—even a better way. What if the welfare of our citizens was handled by the church in America? In ancient Israel, one of the taxes was brought to the local synagogue. The religious leaders received a 3.33 percent tax each year—actually 10 percent every third year (Deuteronomy 14:28)—to care for the needy.

Nowhere in the Bible is the government authorized to take from the rich to give to the poor nor to redistribute wealth. And nowhere in the Bible does the government have the primary responsibility of caring for the poor. The people of God do. What would happen if a 3.33 percent tax (or, like the Bible, a 10 percent every third year) were given to the biblically-grounded faith communities in America? What a joy it would be to see so many receive localized, compassionate, and personalized help they need and deserve.

FAIR TAX OR FLAT TAX?

That brings us back to the original question: is there a certain tax rate that is more biblical than the other ones? One of the advantages of a fair tax is that the government would know much less about our personal incomes. The consumption tax is a user tax. You would pay tax on anything you buy, as opposed to paying on your income. However, God's pattern of taxation, the tithe, is based on one's productivity, not on one's spending.

Having said that I would advocate—due to the biblical model—for a flat tax, a set percentage for every person.

CONCLUSION

In all candor, it is difficult to state unequivocally that the Bible explicitly advocates a specific tax plan, because it does not. As noted in another chapter, we know that the temple and synagogue system of ancient Israel called for three assessments:

- First, a 10 percent tax (local storehouse).
- For taxation purposes, we would not include the "second tithe," another 10 percent, which was set aside, as it was a type of forced savings for religious pilgrimages to Jerusalem.
- An additional 3.33 percent (for the poor) would have been more comparable to our current understanding of taxation.

Allow me to go out on a limb and—in a perfect world, which we do not have—propose a taxation rate as follows:

- **Poll tax:** The ancient head tax or a poll tax could be instituted in which every able-bodied person would participate—the same as was followed by the Israelites during the Exodus. Since it was a male patriarchal system in the Old Testament, allow us, in the interest of equal rights, to include females in this tax. Rather than begin at the age of 20, let us delay it by one year to 21, which allows time for college education, and also because 21 is often regarded as entrance to adulthood. Approximately 70 percent of the population is over 21,[12] which is approximately 220 million out of 320 million. What would the advantages be to *everyone paying something*? All would feel the pride of participation, reducing the entitlement mentality that plagues America. It would be a sufficiently low tax, as the Scriptures stated that even the poor could pay it. I am going to arbitrarily pick 1 percent of one's income, or it could be a flat annual amount, such as $250 (1 percent of $25,000). Imagine the tremendous value of *everyone paying something*, as opposed to the inequities of 50 percent carrying the other half of the population.

- **10 percent flat tax:** In addition to the poll tax, what if the government *would return to exercising only its powers enumerated in the Constitution?* It would need only a fraction of its current budget. With that in mind, every person would pay 10 percent of their income to taxes, a flat tax. The government would receive the same as God taxes, a tithe.
- **3.33 percent:** And what if—as noted above—a 3.33 percent annual income tax, a concept borrowed from ancient Israel's care for the poor, was instituted *locally* for welfare programs for the truly needy.
- **10 percent non-taxed savings:** And let's talk about the second 10 percent tithe of ancient Israel that was mentioned above, used as a type of forced savings. According to the Constitution, our federal government has no legal right to force people to save money. But the government could incentivize savings and wise financial planning by *not* taxing up to 10 percent of one's income—neither on the front end (when received/earned) nor on the back end (when spent/taken out). In other words, this second 10

percent, if placed in self-managed, private savings, would never be taxed. This would result in considerably larger percentages of Americans being able to care for themselves in their elderly years. It would also be in the best interest of our families and communities that people be able to provide for themselves.

Scripture says that we as Christians are to be examples to others by being cheerful givers, since "whoever sows sparingly will also reap sparingly, and whoever sows bountifully will also reap bountifully. Each one must give as he has made up his mind, not reluctantly or under compulsion, for God loves a cheerful giver. And God is able to make all grace abound to you, so that having all sufficiency in all things at all times, you may abound in every good work" (2 Corinthians 9:6–8). This is God's pattern to provide for those in need and to show compassion for others as abundantly as He continues to show to us. If we had a government that was truly responsible in its expenditures, we could have a population that pays it taxes with a considerably improved attitude.

This attitude of giving is in keeping with Matthew 22:39 where we are told to love our neighbor. In the Old Testament we also see acts of help in allowing gleaning (Leviticus 23:22) from one's fields and paying a day's wages for a day's work immediately (Deuteronomy 24:14–15). Throughout the Bible, God's people are to provide for the poor and the downtrodden, independent of any government activity.

In order to fix our broken systems, our government would need to understand that acknowledging the need for God in government does not comprise establishment of religion. It merely establishes integrity, righteousness, and appropriate conduct.

To quote U.S. Senate Chaplain Barry Black at the "Washington— A Man of Prayer" event in Statuary Hall of the U.S. Capitol Building in May of 2012, "We have no problem in Washington, D.C., that prayer cannot solve." That is even true in finding an equitable tax plan and properly handling expenditures.

CHAPTER FIFTEEN

DEBT

Avoid likewise the accumulation of debt, not only by shunning occasions of expense, but by vigorous exertion in time of peace to discharge the debts which unavoidable wars may have occasioned, not ungenerously throwing upon posterity the burden which we ourselves ought to bear... You should practically bear in mind that towards the payment of debts there must be revenue....[1]

—GEORGE WASHINGTON, FAREWELL ADDRESS, 1796

Gather in, kids, the dad hollers out the back door, calling his family from outside. We are going to have a family meeting, he declares. The kids have heard Dad give the "State of the Family" speech before, so they roll their eyes, gathering once again around the kitchen table. Today we are talking about our finances, informs Dad. This family meeting is going to be even more boring than they had imagined.

"Here are the facts," Dad announces. "Our total family income is $52,000 a year, which is average in America today."

"Okay," the four kids respond, each thinking that $52,000 sounds like a lot of money.

"And we are spending $60,800 a year."

135

"Wow," says Junior, the oldest, "that means we are going in the hole $8,800 a year? How do we live?"

"Oh, it is easy, Son. We put it on our credit card." The younger children all nod affirmatively, thinking that since Dad said it, it must be okay.

"But wait," says Junior, "have we been doing that for a long time?"

"Yes."

"But in that Family Life & Planning class I took last year, we had to prepare a mock family budget and plan so that we spent less than we took in."

"Yes," Dad responded, so proud that his son really understood economics.

"But Dad, you just said we are spending more each year than we have income. How long have we been doing that?"

"For decades, Son."

"So, how much do we owe?" asked Junior nervously.

"We have $308,000 on our credit card as of last month's bill," was Dad's carefree response.

"Well, Dad…uh, how do we pay that back?"

"Don't worry, Son, we are in the exact same position as the federal government. You don't see the president worrying about it, do you?"

"But my friend got a D in that class, because his budget spent way more than the family income. The teacher told him that that is a bad thing."

"Don't worry. Your mom and I will be fine."

"But Dad, who will pay it back?" Junior inquired.

"Well, family, that is why I called all of you together. You will!"

"Wait, Dad, are you saying that you and Mom ran up this debt, and you are dumping it on us?"

"Exactly."

What kind of a father would do that to his family? A very selfish one. The family figures given above are, according to the Heritage Foundation, comparable with our federal government debt, except that was in 2014, and it has gotten considerably worse since.[2]

IRRESPONSIBLE AND UNPATRIOTIC

Barack Obama agrees. Or at least *agreed*. Campaigning in 2008, Obama rightly condemned George Bush for taking the national cumulative debt of $5 trillion—from all the previous presidents—and running up another $4 trillion, for a staggering total of $9 trillion. What did Obama call Bush for doing this? Irresponsible and unpatriotic.

Obama stated, "The problem is that the way Bush has done it over the last eight years is to take out a credit card from the Bank of China in the name of our children, driving up our national debt from $5 trillion for the first forty-two presidents. Number forty-three added $4 trillion by his lonesome, so that we now have over $9 trillion of debt that we are going to have to pay back—$30,000 for every man, woman and child. That's irresponsible. It's unpatriotic."[3]

And Obama was correct. But what has he, Barack Obama, done during his presidency? Doubled the debt from $10 trillion to $20 trillion.[4] If what Bush did was irresponsible and unpatriotic, what is this?

Interestingly, the defenders of Obama would have us believe Obama has not really increased the debt. And they scoff at the family illustration, claiming that a government budget is not like a family budget. Let's grant that there might be differences. What does not change, however, is that no one can continually spend more than he makes. Eventually the economic bridge will collapse under the weight of debt, and wise are the people who understand that fact.

When a government refuses to restrain an immense, unpayable debt, it dooms its country's economic well-being. Don't think this can happen? Remember the Weimar Republic after World War I? Germany was in such economic debt that hyper-inflation rendered the currency of the day virtually worthless.[5]

America's debt is—as of the time of this writing—above $19 trillion, moving towards $20 trillion.[6] To put this number into perspective—if we were to divide the debt by the number of people living in the United States, it would amount to $59,000 per person and $160,000 per tax-paying citizen, which would mean an average household debt of two working individuals would amount to an astounding $320,000.[7]

Obama has taken irresponsible and unpatriotic to a terrifying new level.[8]

MORAL AND BIBLICAL ISSUE

Bush added more than $4 trillion, while Obama has more than doubled that, adding almost $10 trillion to the debt. Both presidents were in the wrong. Both signed off on spending way more than America could budget, and left a burden for future generations to carry.

The Bible is clear about this. It says, "You shall not steal" (Exodus 20:15). That not only applies to us today, but it also means we should not steal from future generations. The presidents and the Congress, by running up unsustainable, unpayable debt, have stolen the future of our young adults and children. It is wrong. It is sin. *The national debt has become a moral, theological, biblical issue. Every pulpit in America ought to call out our national leaders for this sin.* The greatest greed is not on Wall Street. It is in Washington, D.C.

What percentage of the Members of Congress attend a Bible-teaching church? One congressman told me 20 percent. That means 80 percent are not in a biblically-centered church. But for the 20 percent that presumably *do* attend such a church, how many of those hear their pastor preach sermons on the moral, theological and biblical underpinnings of our nation's economics? Probably very few. Maybe none.

These otherwise good and sane men and women, our congressional members, continually approve budgets that are spending us into economic oblivion. It is irresponsible. It is immoral. It is called sin. Yet how can we possibly expect the members of Congress to do what is right if pastors will not address this from the pulpit? How can we possibly expect parishioners to consider this issue in the voting booth if their pastor fails to speak on it from the pulpit? The Apostle Paul, speaking of disseminating the truth, raised a good question: "And how can they hear without someone preaching to them?" (Romans 10:14).

Pastors do not need to become more political. They need to become more biblical. The Bible has many verses that speak to economics, whether it is the economics of a family, the government, or any entity.

The good news is that there are those in Congress who *do* care about economic integrity, and they are fighting to correct this. Nevertheless, they are still too few. Similarly, too few preachers are willing to preach about this topic. This is the classic case of sinning by omission that James 4:17 (ESV) warns about: "Whoever knows the right thing to do and fails to do it, for him it is sin." We need pastors, the voters and the elected to become more *well-versed*, to understand that this obscene debt will someday profoundly injure our nation, our children, and our future.

BRIBERY AND GREED

The reason why our debt towers so high is actually quite simple. Politicians bribe the American people—with their own tax money— to expand government programs. It has been said, "The American

Republic will endure until the day Congress discovers that it can bribe the public with the public's money."[9]

BACK TO THE PULPIT

I tried to convey this message once at a pastor's conference. Some looked at me and said, "That's too political; why would we care about the national debt?" I attempted to make the case that this was ultimately not political, but biblical. Sure, it has implication for the political realm, but at its core the issue of debt—national or personal—is a moral, ethical, biblical issue. If I run up a high debt, someone is going to have to pay for what I have done. And that is theft.

America's pastors will need courage to make the sin of massive national debt known. Apathy rages amongst our citizens since the threat of catastrophic consequences seems so far off. Pastors need to instill a sense of urgency about the issue and a strong sense of morality to buck the tide of entitlement mentality and once again reintroduce into the American consciousness a sense of frugality, discipline and restraint.

President Obama is correct. The amount of national debt run up under George W. Bush was unpatriotic. I would add immoral and unethical. And then doubling that debt by Obama is even more unpatriotic, immoral and unethical. Our government is setting an incredibly poor example for its citizens by showing actual and true contempt for the wealth of its citizens and the devastating impact this wastefulness has on industry, initiative, and family welfare.

EARNINGS, DEBT, AND WORK

There are, of course, acceptable instances of debt—unforeseen hospital healthcare emergencies, for example. Most of us have

debt on our house, cars, and in school loans. The Bible never explicitly says debt is forbidden, but issues clear warnings against the
danger of debt. The truth is, "the borrower is servant to the lender"
(Proverbs 22:7).

And we are a debtor's nation. We are becoming the servant to the
nations (China, for example) from which we borrow. In addition, our
children and grandchildren will become the slaves of those who own
their financial notes. This is an untenable situation.

Debt becomes wrong when it burdens future generations. Those
who have allowed the debt situation to spiral will suffer none of the
consequences, as the next generations will have to pay the debt. The
biblical lesson is this: being presumptuous on the future will have a
devastating impact on us as a nation and as families. James 4:14 warns
that we do not know what the future holds. Why, you do not even
know what will happen tomorrow.

Let us state the issue positively. Paying one's debt is biblical. Does
our government have any intention of paying off its obligations? If
not, then it is incredibly ungodly and untrustworthy. Psalms 37:21
states, "The wicked borrow and do not repay."

No country has the authority to take money that people need to
provide for their own families, while the government squanders it on
useless and counterproductive activities. Scripturally, government is
to only take that which is needed for it to perform its fundamental,
biblical role of executing justice against evil-doers and encouraging
the growth of good (Romans 13:4). How much of the annual federal
budget would fall into either of these two categories?

What if we first saved the money, then made a purchase? Whatever happened to earning the money to pay for something ahead of
time, being patient, being appreciative of what has been worked for?
1 Timothy 6:6–9 says, "But godliness with contentment is great gain.
For we brought nothing into the world, and we can take nothing out
of it. But if we have food and clothing, we will be content with that.
Those who want to get rich fall into temptation and a trap and into

many foolish and harmful desires that plunge people into ruin and destruction."

Debt allows us to enjoy things sooner than if we had to work hard for them first, but having debt doesn't allow for the risk associated with unforeseen major problems that may impact us. To run up consumer debt, that is, on depreciating items, is to presume on the future. What is true in the life of an individual is true of a nation. Wise investment is to be praised, as Jesus himself taught in the Parable of the talents (Matthew 25:14–30), but squandering wealth or excessive spending—beyond one's income—is never biblically promoted or encouraged.

Massive national debt isn't biblical. It is morally wrong. Our leaders are squandering the people's wealth. When this happens, the people groan (Proverbs 29:2), and that groaning will grow until responsible men and women, both at a government level and at a personal level, become good stewards again.

CHAPTER SIXTEEN

WELFARE AND WORKFARE

The black family survived centuries of slavery and generations of Jim Crow, but it has disintegrated in the wake of the liberals' expansion of the welfare state.[1]

—THOMAS SOWELL

On the one hand we have got to ask, are there some areas of universal benefits that are no longer affordable? But on the other hand let us look at the issue of dependency where we have trapped people in poverty through the extent of welfare that they have.

—DAVID CAMERON, PRIME MINISTER OF THE UNITED KINGDOM

No one begrudges helping a person in need. Americans are generous. They want to help those legitimately in need. But the definitive word is *legitimately*. Consider these facts:

- Illinois was spending more than $12 million in Medicaid payments for dead people.
- Pennsylvania gave welfare to millionaire lottery winners.
- One hundred percent of reviewed cases in Nebraska's Health Insurance Premium Payment program were missing documents. They found 75 percent of the cases

RACISM, JUDICIAL AND PRISON REFORM

I have a dream that my four little children will one day live in a nation where they will not be judged by the color of their skin but by the content of their character.[1]

—MARTIN LUTHER KING JR.

As I walked out the door toward the gate that would lead to my freedom, I knew if I didn't leave my bitterness and hatred behind, I'd still be in prison.[2]

—NELSON MANDELA

I am an evangelical (although that word has become so diluted that I am not sure if I should use it anymore). We evangelicals are quick to understand that abortion is murder. Presuming we are *well versed*, we understand that the practice of homosexual behavior is sin. But we often fail to address many of the other issues that form the chapters in this book. For example, one of the greatest needs in America today is still racial reconciliation.

In contrast to all the other chapters, I am choosing to be autobiographical on this topic. The scriptural foundations are that all are created equal, in the image of God (Genesis 1:26–27; Galatians 3:28), that we are to love one another (John 13:34), that God shows no favoritism (Acts 10:34), and that while there are different ethnicities, there is only one race, the human race.

"YOU DON'T KNOW ANYTHING"

I am a white person. I grew up in rural Kansas. I never knew any black people as a child. In the closest town, there was one black person in the four-hundred-student high school. I feel like the least qualified person to write a chapter on this topic. But something happened to me that changed my perspective.

In January, 2015, I received an invitation to attend a special conference in Dallas—"The Reconciled Church"—hosted by two of America's great heroes and prophets: Bishop Harry Jackson and Bishop T. D. Jakes. I really wanted to learn from my black brothers, but I was painfully aware that I could contribute so little. My wife and I flew to Dallas. As we landed, I sensed the spirit of God say to me: "You are to say nothing. You don't know anything. You are going to learn. Be silent."

The meeting lasted all day. I recognized quickly that I truly *did* know nothing. I was there to try to grasp the thinking of African Americans who knew the topic not by mere study, but by painful personal experiences. Calling the meeting together, Bishop T. D. Jakes was bold and straightforward. He and the rest of us were not there to state some platitudes about racial unity and then go glibly back home. The conference was a day of learning for me. Later that day, I had an unanticipated chance to be alone with the co-convener, Bishop Jakes. What he shared with me broke my heart.

He reported that over the decades, whites had frequently called on him to support their causes. And he had always responded. "But I always *had to go to them*," he continued. "I am fifty-seven years of age, and this is the first time that whites *have come to us*—as blacks— to support what *we* are doing." The pathos of his story left me deeply moved and quite speechless. I asked him to share his account again with a white brother who was nearby. But the man, oblivious to the deep vulnerability of the moment, interrupted Bishop Jakes, "You know I am not that way." Bishop Jakes nodded in general agreement. I stepped in, "No, listen to what he is saying." Bishop Jakes began again, but, again, he was unsuccessful in completing his story.

I walked away doubly stunned. Not only had a black man trusted me enough to share his pain, but I watched as an otherwise wonderful white brother totally missed the moment. He heard but did not feel the deep wounding of Bishop Jakes. My eyes were opened wider.

Later that evening, about five thousand people gathered at Bishop Jakes's auditorium. I was quite surprised to be asked to share for a few moments along with several others. One great preacher after another spoke, bringing the crowd to its feet. Finally, it was my turn. I explained to the crowd that I had not come to speak, and that I was unworthy to be on the platform. The Holy Spirit had (rightfully) informed me that I knew nothing, was to be silent, and to learn from those who knew. I then simply told four stories about moments that had shaped my understanding of the need for racial healing.

STORY ONE: CONTACTS

My wife Carol was diagnosed in 2007 with primary peritoneal carcinoma, a rare and lethal form of ovarian cancer. For six long and painful years, we went to many places seeking treatment. At one point, just as she was to receive treatment, her lab work came back, and her levels were 1/100th of a point off, throwing her out of the clinical trial. We were told to fly back home, but I knew she needed immediate help.

At that moment, a nationally known professor from a nearby university called me to see how things were going. I explained our dilemma. He happened to know the head of the cancer center and promised to pull a few strings. In the meantime, I called one of the nation's best-known and most highly visible politicians in Washington, D.C. Because of him and his many contacts, Carol was immediately qualified for another clinical trial.

Instead of gloating over my great networking, I sat there exhausted and saddened. I thought of all the people who didn't have the contacts I did. Although I was happy my wife was back in the treatment, I grieved for the people who languish because they lack the connections. As I stood that night at the racial reconciliation conference in front of a crowd that was 90 percent black, I did not have to illustrate the point any further. They understood. Many of them knew what it was like *not* to have friends in high places.

What is the scriptural principle? "As you did it for the least of these, my brothers, you did it for me" (Matthew 25:40, ESV). Look for the "least."

STORY TWO: A DADDY

I told the story of what had happened in that same city, some twenty-four years earlier. My wife Carol and I had adopted four children. One of them perplexed us, and by age four we took him to a pediatric neurologist to help us understand what was going on.

After examining our son, the doctor spoke these crushing words, pointing to our precious child, "This is who comprises the prison population." We were shocked. As I drove the freeway home that day, I asked myself some questions. Knowing my son's learning challenges, what chance did he have? How can he be responsible for himself? Theologians use a fancy word to describe being responsible for a wrong action. It is called culpability. I thought to myself, *How can the men in prison be culpable if they are there because of the way they were born?* It jolted me, as I did not have an answer. I would never view prison the same.

I continued my story that night with these words, "From that day to the present, I have, as a dad, done everything I can possibly do, to make certain my son never does anything to merit prison. But what has plagued my thinking these twenty-four years is this: *What about the little boy who doesn't have a daddy? What chance does he have?*" The reaction of the crowd told me they knew exactly what I was saying.

What is the scriptural principle? God is a "father to the fatherless" (Psalms 68:5, NIV), and as such, we should care as well.

STORY THREE: THEIR ISSUES

I had noticed that my friend Dave Welch in Houston, a white Christian leader, had the complete trust of the black pastors of that city. I asked Dave, "How is it you enjoy such a deep, trusting relationship with them?" He did not hesitate in his response, "Because they know *I care about their issues.*" At that moment, I felt convicted by the Holy Spirit. And the crowd again showed that they understood what I was saying: most of us, as whites, do not really understand their issues, and worse yet, most whites don't even *know that they don't know.*

What is the scriptural principle? "He who does not love his brother whom he has seen cannot love God whom he has not seen" (1 John 4:20, ESV). Care about their issues—whomever the "their" is.

STORY FOUR: I NEEDED THAT

It was at this time that I shared what Bishop T. D. Jakes had shared with me that afternoon. I could not put in words how much his statement had impacted and saddened me. I told the crowd that after the Bishop shared with me, I had begun to wonder what the black pastors in San Diego would say about me. I had wondered if they would say, "Jim comes to us." Or would they say, "Jim always expects us to come to him." I did not want to contemplate what the answer might be.

I then looked at Bishop Jakes sitting on the front row, and said, "I am sorry. I am so sorry. Fifty-seven years is too long for you to have to wait. We have done wrong. It has taken us a long time. But we are here with you now. Please forgive me. Please forgive us. We *can* do better. We will *do* better."

What happened next was not planned. The crowd stood to their feet, applauding, cheering, and even crying. I began to walk to my seat. But Bishop Jakes met me first. We embraced and held each other for a long time. The cameras caught the moment. And if anyone looked carefully you could lip read what he is saying, "I needed that. I needed that. I needed that."

What is the scriptural principle? In John 4:4 (AMPC), Jesus decided that "it was necessary for Him to go through Samaria," to intersect with a racially different group. In Luke 10:31–32, the priest and Levite both "passed by on the other side" to avoid going to the place of need. But one man went to the one in need. He did not expect the one in need to come to him. Jesus said, "Go and do likewise" (Luke 10:37, NIV).

REACH OUT AND LEARN

Surveys indicate that America is not moving in the right direction on this issue of race. In 2004, during the George W. Bush administration, 74 percent of whites and 68 percent of blacks thought race relations were "very good" or "somewhat good."[3] Most assumed—including me—that the election of a black president would improve race relations. That did not happen. By 2015, seven years into President Obama's tenure, only 45 percent of whites and 51 percent of blacks agreed race relations were "very good" or "somewhat good."[4] Tragically, racial tensions seem to be increasing. That is why Americans of all colors coming together to listen and to share our burdens, our sorrows, and our lack of understanding is so important, today more than ever.

The key issues that we learned about in "The Reconciled Church" experience were:

- The tragic educational conditions in predominantly black areas
- The absence of economic investment in black areas
- Judicial reform
- Prison reform

I would add the biggest one of all: the destruction of the black family unit. Seven out of ten black children are growing up in a home with no daddy.[5] Not having a married father and mother living together is the greatest predictor of poverty for all children of all ethnicities.[6] These five issues now deeply concern me. I pray they will you as well.

JUDICIAL REFORM

A friend of mine recently got into deep legal trouble. At first, he was going to have a public defender. However, some friends stepped in and paid for a good attorney. As I watched his court case mature, I was stunned at the difference between accused persons who had public defenders and the ones who had a highly qualified attorney. What made the difference? Funds to pay for a good attorney, not to get him off, but to get him a fair sentence that would help him towards becoming a productive citizen.

Leaving the courtroom, we celebrated the legal victory. After walking the long courthouse hallway, however, I realized my wife was not with us. I turned around to find her praying over a young black man who appeared to be about nineteen or twenty years old. I then remembered seeing him while leaving the courtroom. I had passed by oblivious to him. But my wife *really* saw him. She stopped and took quite a bit of time to talk to him, pray for and with him, and just be with him. He was sitting on the floor, awaiting his time before the judge. He had no dad with him. No mother. No family member. No one. I wish now that I knew his name, that I could contact him, pray for him, and find out what I might be able to do to help him.

Many others in the court system, like this young man, have no family, no social support system. What can be done in our churches to construct, under the guidance of the Holy Spirit, a mentoring ministry in which we assign mature church leaders to felons who desire help?

PRISON REFORM

A few years ago, my wife Rosemary (after my wife Carol died, and I went through a season of deep grief, I then remarried) and I were given a tour of the well-known Leavenworth Prison located in my home state of Kansas. We were taken through three large, secured entrances, each time hearing the sound of the gates locking behind us. I expected to see people in cells. That was not the case. The prison was a virtual city. Khaki-clad prisoners were walking freely—to work, to classes, and to school. And the prison guards were unarmed. For sure, the violent offenders were secured in another area; but here we were walking freely as civilians among thousands of prisoners.

We were told about the occasional frightening moments, so I don't want to understate the potential for danger. Yet the fact remains that an extremely high percentage of the inmates were not violent at all, but were in for drug usage. I am not minimizing the danger of drug usage, but one could quickly see that this was not the best use of our tax dollars.

Instead of this catch-and-contain system, we need rehabilitation programs that will truly change people and make them productive. I suspect you have noticed that this chapter is unabashedly autobiographical. That is intentional.

God is convicting me, as a white guy in suburbia, to rethink how I can care about *their* issues and how I might minister to those in prison.

TORI

One of the best ways to reduce the rapidly growing prison population is to construct ministries that help assure that former prisoners do not return. Bishop Jakes's church, The Potter's House in Dallas, is more than a huge church building with a large attendance. It is the place to go when one gets out of prison.

It is quite possible that this one church has established the model for us all, creating a Jesus centered, Holy Spirit-filled, welcoming environment for giving newly released inmates the mind of Christ, and helping us all to properly care for our brothers and sisters in need. The program is called TORI (Texas Offenders Reentry Initiative) and was founded by Bishop T. D. Jakes to bridge economic voids in urban America.

Ex-inmates face insurmountable obstacles upon returning to their communities. Bringing together judges, lawyers, social workers, counselors and business leaders from his congregation, Bishop Jakes formed TORI. Since 2005 it has served over 10,000 formerly incarcerated persons.[7] The congregation has 150 volunteers trained to assist in this ministry. TORI is reducing the rate of recidivism, as it ministers with biblical principles.

TORI offers a one-year case-management program, complete with assessment, intervention plans and goal setting, built around six of the key needs of formerly incarcerated persons:

- Housing—Network of property owners, local shelters, transitional housing programs and the local housing authorities assist clients with independent living.
- Employment—Employment coaching assists clients with job skills, interviewing, resume writing, and job search/placement.
- Education—GED and higher education preparation and career planning, classes/support groups for cognitive behavioral and addiction issues, basic life skills, financial literacy, and empowerment.
- Healthcare—Health education and substance abuse awareness, training, and prevention. Individual and family counseling.
- Family Reunification—Comprehensive intervention to identify family strengths and deficiencies and to increase family functioning level.
- Spiritual—Spiritual guidance, mentoring, spiritual counseling and community service projects.

Case managers invest twelve months in each client, assisting them in setting goals, creating a plan of action, while offering supervision and monitoring to ensure healthy accountability. In addition, they provide training in cognitive behavioral and empowerment classes (employment coaching, anger management, substance abuse, parenting), case management appointments, and assigned monthly community service projects.

"I AM MORE!"

The TORI program encourages clients to adopt the personal mantra, "I am more!" TORI "does not just show ex-offenders how to reintegrate into society but more importantly it helps them identify the propensities, choices, and decisions that brought them to a negative end in the first place," said Bishop T. D. Jakes.[8]

At the completion of the program, each client experiences the joy of a formal graduation ceremony in the Potters House Sunday morning worship service with thousands cheering them on. Criminal Court judges—joined by Bishop Jakes—hand out the certificates of completion instead of sentences to jail, affirming the joyous reality that their past does not define their future.

Does TORI's biblical based strategy work? See for yourself: Recidivism continues to be a problem in the U.S. with 67 percent of former prisoners re-arrested and 52 percent re-incarcerated within three years of their release. The recidivism rate for those who complete the TORI program is only 11 percent.[9] TORI Executive Director Tina Naidoo, ended a recent personal email to me with the words, "We are the voice and the hand that encourages people to change their lives with hope, comfort and peace."[10]

This is the church at work. This is a church that is *well versed*.

A CALL FOR INNER HEALING

On April 9, 2016, Bishop Harry Jackson, along with Bernice King (daughter of Martin Luther King Jr.) and Alveda King (niece of Martin Luther King Jr.), were involved in a public event—United Cry 2016—in front of the Lincoln Memorial in Washington, D.C., to further racial reconciliation. After a time of public repentance for sins of the past and an act of foot washing (sign of humility and repentance), approximately twenty blacks, whites, and Hispanics were presented with specially designed mantles portraying racial reconciliation. I was privileged to be one of the persons to be given a special plaque and small, glass-encased stones from the Lincoln Memorial area where years before Martin Luther King Jr. had stood and spoken. I cannot describe how unworthy I felt that day, to be standing with many blacks who have paid such a high price due to racism. As I stood there among so many whom I respected, I asked God to help me somehow be faithful to the calling to help further racial healing.

There is no doubt that it is a matter of the heart. And Jesus can change a heart. Before we were married in 2014, my wife Rosemary attended a church in Oakland, California, that was likely 75 percent black and pastored by her white son-in-law. In addition, three of her brothers are married to African Americans, another to a Hispanic, and another to a Swedish woman. Why is there no racial strife in this church or in this family? Their hearts were changed by Jesus Christ. Rosemary's church and family don't need racial "reconciliation." They are oblivious to any racial "problems," because of what Christ does to the heart and the depth of loving interracial relationships.

PART VI

FOREIGN POLICY AND WORLD ISSUES

CHAPTER TWENTY-THREE

NATIONAL DEFENSE AND WAR

A universal and perpetual peace, it is to be feared, is in the catalogue of events, which will never exist but in the imaginations of visionary philosophers, or in the breasts of benevolent enthusiasts.[1]

—JAMES MADISON

To be prepared for war is one of the most effectual means of preserving peace.[2]

—GEORGE WASHINGTON

Justified or not, war has been a constant since the fall (Ecclesiastes 3:1, 8). We live in a broken world, and the sinful nature of man and governments virtually guarantees wars will continue until the Lord returns to claim His own (Matthew 24:6–8).

It is naïve to expect to live at peace with other nations that don't share our moral values. In the Cold War following World War II, President Ronald Reagan summarized our guarded relationship with the other world superpower at the time (the atheistic Soviet Union): "Trust, but verify."[3] Strive for peace but always be prepared for war; live up to the age-old adage of "peace through strength."

As an autonomous, sovereign nation, we have the right to defend ourselves from all enemies, foreign and domestic. National sovereignty is a biblical principle established by God. He raises nations up and brings them down (Daniel 2:20–21; Acts 17:24–26); their very existence serves to fulfill His purposes.

War is a particularly vile expression of man's corrupt nature and is ultimately a rejection of God's divine rule. In a real sense, declaring a so-called "war" on drugs, poverty, or crime weakens our perception of the inhumanity of war, as it has slaughtered hundreds of millions of men, women, and children over the millennia.

WHY IS THERE WAR?

War is God's judgment upon the world for rejecting Him and His Son Jesus Christ—the Prince of Peace! The Bible clearly documents God's judgment of even His own chosen people when they became disobedient (Leviticus 26:23–26, 33; Isaiah 1:19–20; Jeremiah 5:14–17; Deuteronomy 28:49–52; etc.). Israel's rejection of the Lordship of God ultimately resulted in utter destruction of their nation by countries even viler than they (Habakkuk 1:1–12). Even more telling is God's use of war as a sign of His judgment in the end times (Revelation 6:3–4).

Are we immune from God's judgment? Of course not! Our nation was born in the bloody Revolutionary War, constituted under God with the means to secure and protect our God-given rights. It took a Civil War to purge our nation of the scourge of slavery. World War I and World War II countered the very real threat of global tyranny and fascism. And in modern times, we have participated in any number of regional wars to protect our national interests and stop the development of regimes willing to use weapons for political and religious domination.

What are the national interests we are trying to protect? They include health, economic, financial, and environmental interests, as well as our way of life, our institutions, our freedoms (liberty with responsibility), our laws, and even our positive influence on the world, originating from our Christian values.

A JUSTIFIED WAR

As a nation with a Christian legacy, our approach to life and death decisions will obviously reflect those values consistent with a biblical worldview. A case in point is that our nation (and only our nation) has spent trillions of dollars to defend not only ourselves but our allies. America has also invested incredible amounts of defense funding in precision weapons and high-tech intelligence instead of relying on brute, crushing force to kill as many people as possible. But when *should* we use lethal force?

The tendency, at least in the Christianized West, has been to limit the extent of war and the methods used to conduct it. Writings on the concept of *just war* began with Augustine and continue today. A just war is a war limited by moral principles and conducted by a legitimate authority. These principles include critically examining whether the causes of war are just, and whether the means used in conducting the war are justified.

Some examples of just reasons for going to war include self-defending against an obvious threat, or our rights, liberties, and government; defending an ally that is unjustly attacked; and even redressing a national wrong. A war waged for selfish gain, self-interest, pure power, or expansion of territory is categorically unjust. Finally, there must be a reasonable prospect of success to wage war. In other words, deaths and injuries for a hopeless cause cannot be morally justified. These values are virtually unknown in the world except among nations with a Christian worldview that values life.

THE CONDUCT OF WAR

First, war must be the last resort. All reasonable, non-violent options must be exhausted before the use of force can be justified; pre-emptive strikes are only justified when there is a clear and present threat.

Second, leaders must discriminate between combatants and non-combatants. It is unjust to target civilians in wartime, or to attack with lethal force indiscriminately. As distasteful as it is, civilian deaths are justifiable only if they are unavoidable victims of a deliberate attack on a military target. Just war principles also call for prisoners and conquered peoples to be treated well and honorably, and that all non-war-related resources be left intact, including life-sustaining resources.

Finally, the use of force must be proportionate. It is unjust to use unnecessary force (wanton violence, unfair brutality, excessive force) to accomplish the objective, or to extend the war after the enemy has been beaten.

A dispassionate look at how our nation has conducted conflict in modern times shows that many of these principles have been followed, sometimes to our own detriment in the face of an enemy who does not abide by the same concern for life.

CHAPTER TWENTY-FOUR

IMMIGRATION AND BORDER SECURITY

But the simple truth is that we've lost control of our own borders, and no nation can do that and survive.[1]

—RONALD REAGAN

I sometimes think it is a good rule of thumb to ask of a country: are people trying to get into it or out of it? It's not a bad guide to what sort of country it is.[2]

—TONY BLAIR

Aren't we all immigrants? Well, yes and no. Some of us are recent immigrants; most of us have immigrants somewhere in our family history. Some have Native American ancestry. But even they trace their ancestry from somewhere else. Other than the original world inhabitants—Adam and Eve in the Garden of Eden (Genesis 2:5–8, 15; somewhere in the pre-flood middle east)—the entire human race is made up of immigrants or the offspring of immigrants. Even with that established, few issues are more divisive than immigration. I will likely frustrate persons on both extremes of this issue.

U.S. ACCEPTANCE OF IMMIGRANTS

There's no other nation more compassionate, more generous, or more open-armed towards the less fortunate nations than the United States. Our Christian heritage has conditioned us to respond to local and global catastrophes remarkably quickly and effectively. We allow more immigrants from all over the world to enter our country than any other nation on earth.[3] Why? Because all people have an intrinsic worth, being made in God's image (Genesis 1:27), independent of race, color, or ethnic background. Those that want to contribute to the American Experiment are welcome to do so, if they support our values, respect our unique religious heritage, and play by the rules. Therefore, understand that the United States should not feel any shame concerning its overall acceptance of immigrants.

BORDERS

National borders help governments establish who is a member (citizen), who is a visitor, and who shouldn't get through the door. This process is similar to church membership. The pastors need to be able to distinguish between who needs to be shepherded and who is just passing through. It doesn't make visitors less important, but membership establishes clear expectations concerning how authority applies, what resources are available for whom, what privileges can be expected, and where attention is to be concentrated. Like a church, a nation has the right to enforce borders and having no borders means it is no longer a nation.

THE FAILURE OF DEMOCRATS AND REPUBLICANS

Sadly, both political sides have little interest in solving our border issue. The Democratic Party is vested in growing dependent classes of people as large as possible to maintain political power through voting influence. It is all about power. Labor unions—overwhelmingly Democratic—were pro-immigration in the early 1900s.[4] They stood to benefit from unskilled workers who would swell their ranks and support their radical causes. But by the end of the 1900s, some labor unions disdained immigrants who took jobs for less pay, driving wages down.[5]

The Republican Party also has strong ties to business interests whose large employers happily accept the cheap labor and rising profits. In addition, they also are afraid of being labeled racist if they crack down on those seeking a better life.

MY PERSONAL LOOK

Several years ago, I attended a special three-day Border School in El Paso, TX. There are twenty-three counties along the U.S.-Mexico border in four states (California, Arizona, New Mexico, and the majority in Texas). We were taught by Zapata County Sheriff, Sigifredo "Sigi" Gonzalez Jr., who founded the Southwestern Border Sheriff's Coalition, and Hudspeth County Sheriff Arvin West and others. We experienced not only classroom time, but we were also taken to the border. Our instruction included a tour of the federally run El Paso Intelligence Center (EPIC).

We saw several hundred disturbing pictures of what was happening at our border. There were stories of rape, torture and murder. There was evidence of OTMs, "other than Mexicans," which actually means "other than Hispanics," coming across the border, specifically immigrants from the Middle East, as Arabic writing was found left behind in the litter.

But the most disturbing thing was this: When the sheriffs from the nation's southwest border counties went to Washington, D.C., to appeal for help, they were denied assistance by both the Bush 43 administration and the Obama administration! These county sheriffs were left on their own to deal with, not just kind Mexicans looking for jobs, but the ruthless and gruesome Mexican drug cartel. Bottom line: both political parties benefit by saying they'll fix the problem but never doing so.

WHAT ABOUT COMPASSION?

If someone came into your home, even someone without a penny to his name, do they have the right to stay indefinitely and take whatever they want? You know the answer. But if you were to leave your windows and doors wide open all day, leave money and fresh food lying around, hang the keys to the car in plain sight, and ignore everyone coming in and out, your home would be packed (and sacked) in no time!

With penalty-free access to open borders, sanctuary cities, unenforced federal laws, driver's licenses, in-state tuition, free medical care, welfare, and any number of other entitlements—even amnesty—what's the incentive to respect our laws, our values, and our heritage? In fact, lawlessness and the abuse of compassion actually breeds a contempt for authority and broad-based resentment toward each other.

Having said that, what kingdom issues are at stake? My own denomination, the Wesleyan Church, has processed eight different principles that form the framework we use to choose a biblical response:

1. **The Creation Principle:** All persons are created equal and are of equal worth in their Creator's eyes.
2. **The Great Commandment Principle:** Christ commands us to love God with all our heart, soul, and mind and our neighbors as ourselves.

3. **The Sovereignty Principle:** God is sovereignly at work to establish His kingdom in heaven and on earth. He determines the times and places where the peoples of the nations should live, so that people will seek Him and perhaps reach out for Him and find Him.
4. **The Submission Principle:** Christians possess dual citizenship, one heavenly and the other earthly. Christians should respect and submit to the laws of the land, except when they are in contradiction to biblical principles.
5. **The Hospitality Principle:** Christ's love compels us to be kind and compassionate and to offer hospitality, especially to those in need, including strangers, widows, orphans, aliens, and immigrants, regardless of their legal status.
6. **The Great Commission Principle:** Jesus Christ brings good news and has commissioned us to make disciples of all peoples, including citizens and aliens alike.
7. **The Grace Principle:** All have sinned and deserve God's judgment and punishment. Yet, He is a merciful God and seeks to reconcile us to Himself by grace.
8. **The Justice Principle:** God's people are called to seek justice for all persons proactively by calling for just, fair, reasonable, and humane laws and serving as advocates and defenders for those who are powerless, disenfranchised, and marginalized.[6]

THE CORE OF THE PROBLEM

If you have ever heard a discussion of these issues, you are familiar with the usual arguments. On one side: *Be reasonable! They are illegals. This issue is cut and dry.*

On the other side: *Be compassionate! They are hard workers, trying to feed their families, and they carry out many jobs that Americans don't want anyway.*

The main culprit in these arguments is the subversive message from our federal government: *We are not going to enforce the law.*[7] When a law is not enforced, it ceases to be a law. The legal term is *desuetude* (pronounced DEH-swah-tude). A law on the books that is not enforced is in desuetude. If law enforcement ignores it, so does everyone else, including the people who now violate the inactive law.

The government should have the integrity to either enforce a law or, if not, follow the proper procedures for removing it. We were taught as children that we are a nation of laws. Laws are not supposed to be on the books but in desuetude. No enforcement? Then remove the laws. And therein lies the heart of the issue. I am a law-and-order guy. But I do not blame those who crossed the border. If I were a father and husband living in central Mexico, without a job to support my family, and I learned that the U.S. government no longer enforced the law, I would cross the border and get a job in the U.S. Why? Because the U.S. government has told me that border enforcement is no longer a law.

The culpability lies in Washington, D.C., in both Republican and Democratic administrations. For their own reasons, each party has violated its obligation to uphold the law of the land. I am personally in favor of a strong border, but if the federal government demonstrates that it has no intention of following its own law, then the people who cross our borders can hardly be blamed. This applies not only to those who crossed illegally but to those (almost 40 percent are undocumented[8]) who overstayed their time in the United States.

So what do we do now that the government has created such a horrific mess? For a church, this is not a problem. Our calling is to evangelize and edify in the name of Christ. We are not a law enforcement agency, although we do attempt to help people submit to the governing authorities. My conservative friends are going to have to swallow hard and accept the fact that these immigrants have been drawn here, in part, by a policy lacking clarity or rather, no policy at all.

TWO HEALING STEPS

There are two necessary steps that will bring our nation towards healing. First, the government needs to acknowledge its failure. Most politicians will blame-shift to those who served in previous years. But here is where healing can occur. Our government—Democrats and Republicans—needs to acknowledge its wrong-doing. This apology is not merely for the government's legal self-nullification, but for its failure to adequately protect the nation. While you might contend this will never occur, it already has happened and can happen again.[9]

Second, immigrants have a role to play. What about the ones who crossed the border and are now here illegally? Yes, fines should be paid. Yes, back taxes must be paid. Yes, papers must be appropriately filed. Yes, the English language must be taught. Yes, U.S. history and citizenship classes need to be taken (ones that truly affirm America's rich heritage). Yes, allegiance to America needs to be confirmed while renouncing any other allegiances. Yes, compliance with our laws needs to be ongoing. Yes, full assimilation into American values needs to be completed. But *no*, they should not be deported to their native country, given the fact that our government openly negated its own law. *This is not amnesty.* Amnesty is only winking at a violation. There is a massive difference between granting amnesty and creating a *pathway*.

Without question, there needs to be a larger debate on who should be permanently allowed into our country and under what conditions. But in coming here, it must be understood all are to cherish what we stand for as a nation. They must understand and respect our national foundation as being based on eternal Judeo-Christian values and morals. They must commit to working hard to provide for themselves, their families and the continued prosperity, unity and common good of this country. Just as the exiles were told by Jeremiah to be a blessing to the land they were going to, so those who enter the United States are to have the same attitude (Jeremiah 29:7).

OFFENDING EVERYONE

While I have offended everyone on the Right by now, I might as well offend everyone on the Left, too. Progressives appeal to emotions on this issue. They need to stop. Their guilt games and gross misuse of Scripture only muddy the waters of an already complicated issue. One of President Obama's most flagrant abuses of Scriptures was his comparison, during the Christmas season of 2014, of Joseph and the Virgin Mary as "visitors" in Bethlehem, to illegal immigrants being "visitors" in America. No, Mr. President, Joseph and Mary were not visitors. Rather, they were returning to their own ancestral hometown (Luke 2:3). They were not there illegally.[10]

Remarkably, Obama does not cite Scripture when it defines marriage as one man–one woman (Genesis 2:24; Matthew 19:4–6), or when it speaks of life in the womb (Psalms 139:13–14; Jeremiah 1:5). But when he wants to make his case for executive orders to promote immigration, he suddenly becomes Preacher-in-Chief: "Scripture tells us that we shall not oppress a stranger, for we know the heart of a stranger—we were strangers once, too," said Obama citing Exodus 22:21.[11] There is a small problem with his use of the text: it doesn't apply. The word for stranger or alien in the Hebrew is *ger*. The word actually refers to one "who had entered Israel and followed legal procedures to obtain recognized standing as a resident alien."[12]

These verses so often used by the Left about sojourners, strangers, and aliens refer to *legal* immigrants who have recognized standing. Those who were in Israel without legal standing were described by another Hebrew word that translated as *foreigners*.[13] Obama's use of the biblical text actually refers to people who were in compliance with national law, not in violation of it.

Those on the Left seem oblivious to the reality that some would-be immigrants should not be allowed in. Some are dangerous. They steal, rape and murder. They are bad people! Typical of the Left, politicians deny the existence of evil and the reality that Jihadi cells can be concealed amongst immigrants and refugees. The irony is that these leaders would never invite an armed robber into their home to steal, plunder, rape and kill. Yet, on a much larger scale, they want Americans to do exactly that. That is naïve, hypocritical, and it endangers us all.

Since the role of the government is to protect the citizenry, the government is morally, biblically, and constitutionally obligated to have a vetting process that is so thorough that it weeds out all who would do harm. Having special protections in place for keeping terrorists from taking advantage of our porous southern border is not xenophobic. It is smart. And it is necessary.

CHAPTER TWENTY-FIVE

ISRAEL

*I will insist the Hebrews have [contributed] more to civilize
men than any other nation. If I was an atheist and believed
in blind, eternal fate, I should still believe that fate had
ordained the Jews to be the most essential instrument for
civilizing the nations… They are the most glorious nation
that ever inhabited this Earth. The Romans and their
empire were but a bubble in comparison to the Jews.*[1]

—JOHN ADAMS

*In Israel, in order to be a realist, you must believe
in miracles.*[2]

—DAVID BEN-GURION

O f the nearly two hundred nations on the earth, why is a tiny one,
no bigger than the state of New Jersey, consistently in the national
news? Of all the other nations of the earth, this is the only one
that gets its own chapter in this book. Why an entire chapter about
this one small country?

I once had a conversation in Washington, D.C., as I sat in the
office of one of the members of the U.S. House of Representatives,
asking how I could pray for him. In the course of the conversation he
unexpectedly asked, "Aren't we supposed to support Israel? Where is
that in the Bible?" I laid out one Bible verse after another. He immediately got a paper and pencil and began writing each verse down.

Later that night, I saw him again and said, "Congressman, when we were talking, I forgot the most important verse about our support of Israel." He grabbed the well-used, folded paper from his pocket and prepared to write. "Genesis 12:3 is the most important one," I continued, "which says 'I will bless those who bless you (speaking of Israel), and whoever curses you I will curse....'"

Years ago, I served on the board of Christ for the Nations Institute in Dallas—the flagship of some fifty different Bible Colleges around the globe—led by the remarkable Freda Lindsey. At the beginning of each school year she would stand before the student body and ask, "Who wants to be blessed?" All hands went up. "And who wants to be cursed?" No hands. The key to blessings, she would explain, is to bless Israel.

Too simplistic? Not at all. Genesis 12:3 summarizes it well. Bless Israel, be blessed. Curse Israel, be cursed. Which do you prefer?

Of course, this does not mean that the state of Israel always makes the right decisions. It does not mean that we despise people of Arabic descent. Then, what does *blessing Israel* mean? Blessing Israel means affirming the scriptural reality that God loves the land and the state of Israel. He has not turned His back on this piece of real estate. Yes, God loves *all* people, but the Jewish people and the state of Israel have a special place in God's unfolding plan. Israel is where the Messiah came. To Israel is where He will return. In Israel is where He will set up His Kingdom, not in New York City, London, or Paris; it will be in Jerusalem.

THE REGATHERING

Israel was destroyed and its people scattered in AD 70 when Jerusalem was sacked by the Romans. Miraculously, they slowly began regathering, with the help of Christians, in the 1800s, followed by the official beginning of the Zionist Movement in 1897 by Theodore

Herzl. Fifty-one years later, the nation was reborn—in a day—just as God said it would be. Isaiah 66:8 states, "Who has ever heard of such a thing? Who has ever seen such things? Can a country be born in a day or a nation be brought forth in a moment?"

Not only was the nation born in a day, May 14, 1948, but Jews began returning in greater numbers, particularly after the Holocaust. As Isaiah verse 66:8 continues, "Yet no sooner is Zion in labor than she gives birth to her children." No nation has ever disappeared for two thousand years and then come back into existence. But we should not be surprised. God had foretold it:

- Ezekiel 20:34: "I will bring you from the nations and gather you from the countries where you have been scattered-with a mighty hand and an outstretched arm and with outpoured wrath."
- Ezekiel 34:13: "I will bring them out from the nations and gather them from the countries, and I will bring them into their own land. I will pasture them on the mountains of Israel, in the ravines and in all the settlements in the land."
- Isaiah 43:5–6: "Do not be afraid, for I am with you; I will bring your children from the east and gather you from the west. I will say to the north, 'Give them up!' and to the south, 'Do not hold them back.' Bring my sons from afar and my daughters from the ends of the earth."
- Amos 9:14–15: "'I will bring back my exiled people Israel; they will rebuild the ruined cities and live in them. They will plant vineyards and drink their wine; they will make gardens and eat their fruit. I will plant Israel in their own land, never again to be uprooted from the land I have given them,' says the Lord your God."

Not only was a nation reborn, but the defunct language, Hebrew, was reinstituted, along with Jewish currency, the shekel.

ZIONISM DEFINED

A Zionist is one who believes that Israel has a right to exist and to defend itself. Nothing more. Nothing less. Consequently, a Christian Zionist is simply a follower of Jesus who believes that Israel has the right to exist and to defend itself. Due to Scripture's teaching on the Jewish people and Israel, I am a Christian Zionist.

In case you don't see yourself as a Zionist, let me ask you a question. Do you believe that America has a right to exist? Do you believe that Americans have a right to defend themselves from people who want to kill them?

The same rights should be true for Israel, the only democracy in the entire Middle East and—for the record—the only place where Christians are protected.

HISTORIC CHRISTIAN ANTI-SEMITISM

After the time of Christ, the early Church grew rapidly, consisting of both Jewish and Gentile believers. Within three hundred years, Christianity blanketed the Roman Empire so heavily that Christianity—under Emperor Constantine—became the established religion of the entire Empire. After that, came a purge of anything Jewish. The ancient Jewish festivals were replaced by Easter and Christmas. Forms of liturgy and worship became distinctly Roman in an attempt to remove all things Jewish.

During these centuries another vitriolic myth arose—that the Jews killed Jesus. There were *some* Jews and *some* Romans (Gentiles) involved in the crucifixion of Christ. (But in reality, *our* sins caused the death of Jesus. His death on the cross was God's plan from the beginning—per Genesis 3:15—to bring a solution to sin and salvation to humankind.) Early church fathers who gave many great teachings to the church, began to write viciously regarding the Jewish people. John Chrysostom, the golden-mouthed orator of Christianity in his time, most unfortunately contributed to the hatred of Jews.[3]

The Middle Ages did not improve Christian-Jewish relations. Perhaps the most tragic of all was the year 1099, when allegedly Christian Crusaders locked nine hundred and sixty-nine Jewish men, women, and children in a Jerusalem synagogue and set it on fire while marching around singing, "Christ we adore Thee!" *Kill a Jew and save your soul* became one of the Crusader battle cries.[4]

Even one of the great heroes of the church, Martin Luther, would write negatively regarding the Jews.[5] Adolf Hitler would read these words centuries later and twist them into something worse—the cremation of six million Jews as alleged Christian doctrine!

REPLACEMENT THEOLOGY

But an even more sophisticated theological form of anti-Semitism developed. A teaching arose called replacement theology, meaning that all the Old Testament promises were no longer for Israel, but for the Christian church. After all, centuries passed, and no Israel had formed and no Jews had re-gathered.

Then, in one of the most stunning turn of events, the state of Israel was born. Not only born, but birthed in a single day, just like Scripture promised in Isaiah 66:8. President Harry S. Truman—against the advice of his counselors—remembering his Sunday School studies of King Cyrus (who allowed the Jews to return to their land from Persia), declared himself a modern Cyrus and recognized the state of Israel only eleven minutes after it declared itself a nation, on May 14, 1948.[6] Within hours, five Arab nations declared war on the infant state.[7] And the attempt to rob the Jews of their homeland has continued ever since.

With the miraculous establishment of Israel came the equally miraculous increase in the flow of Jews back to Israel from all over the globe, precisely as prophesied. These are only two of the many biblical promises of the regathering of the Jews to Israel:

- Ezekiel 36:24: "For I will take you from the nations, gather you from all the lands and bring you into your own land."
- Ezekiel 37:21–23: "Say to them, 'Thus says the Lord God, "Behold, I will take the sons of Israel from among the nations where they have gone, and I will gather them from every side and bring them into their own land; and I will make them one nation in the land, on the mountains of Israel; and one king will be king for all of them; and they will no longer be two nations and no longer be divided into two kingdoms.... And they will be My people, and I will be their God.'"

This fulfilled prophecy made it particularly embarrassing for those advocating replacement theology or its sidekick, fulfillment theology, the view that Christ somehow fulfilled prophecy in such a way that God no longer cares about Israel.

With each passing day, more and more of ancient biblical prophecies are being fulfilled. Allow me to mention only one very briefly which I have personally witnessed. Jeremiah 31:5–6 states, "Again you will plant vineyards on the hills of Samaria; the farmers will plant them and enjoy their fruit. There will be a day when watchmen cry out on the hills of Ephraim, 'Come, let us go up to Zion, to the Lord our God.'"

For thousands of years the hills of Samaria—under the Arab leadership in what is commonly called "the West Bank"—lie in desolation.

But this Scripture states that this badly eroded land will be covered with vineyards—with "watchmen."

After 2,700 years, this prophecy is being fulfilled right now. Under the leadership of Tommy Waller (of Tennessee, USA), the horribly eroded soil of the hills of Samaria are being tenderly cultivated. Teams of people—Christians from the USA—are volunteering their time—at their expense—to go live there and plant, cultivate, and harvest the vineyards for the Jewish farmers. Experts at a respected university had informed them after testing a soil sample that this land would never be able to produce. But Jeremiah had prophesied otherwise. Not only did it produce, but the wine from these grapes was entered in an international competition in Paris and won first place.

And what about the *watchmen* that Jeremiah spoke about? The transliterated word is "notzriym" (pronounced "notes-REEM"). In modern Hebrew, that is the word for Christians. In other words, almost three millennia ago, Jeremiah said that the "notzriym," or "Christians," would come to the hills of Samaria and "farmers" would plant vineyards. And they did! One of the most delightful moments of our many trips to Israel was the moment we arrived at HaYovel just in time for the final moments of the grape harvest. They handed us clippers to join the group as we all harvested the final grapes of the season and a grand, explosive festival of joy broke out!

BDS: MORE ANTI-SEMITISM

The attacks on modern day Israel never end. One of the most inexplicable and logic-lacking attacks on Israel is the BDS movement. BDS stands for "boycott" (Israel's products), "divest" (on any investments in Israel) and "sanction" (ban on trade or participation with Israel in any way). Leaders of this misguided and historically ignorant movement overwhelmingly have no problem affirming terrorist nations such as Iran or North Korea, and even fail to condemn random Palestinian acts of violence against innocent Israeli civilians. At the core, this is one more in a very long line of anti-Semitic rants.

Many university campuses and left-wing groups are fanning the flames of hatred through the BDS movement. Time and space limits us to giving only one example, the severely anti-scriptural Presbyterian Church USA—the PCUSA (not to be confused with the biblical and smaller denomination known as the Presbyterian Church of America, PCA). In 2014 the unhinged PCUSA voted not merely to support BDS, but to—get this—vote on removing the word "Israel" from its prayers and hymns, lest this might imply support for modern Israel.[8] No proclamation was made against terrorist nations. PCUSA officials however had no problem fraternizing with known Hezbollah terrorists who have some two hundred thousand rockets readied to unload on Israel, when the moment is right.

REPEATED ATTEMPTS TO DESTROY ISRAEL

What about the ongoing conflict in Israel? After all, didn't Israel take land from the Palestinians? Let's be clear. Israel is not occupying the land. Israel owns it. God—who owns the whole earth—gave it to the Jewish people.

This is only a partial list of the attacks upon Israel and/or the offensive actions that the Israeli Defense Forces have had to take in order to defend their nation:

- Israeli War of Independence (November 1947–July 1949)
- Suez Crisis (October 1956)
- Six-Day War (June 1967)—Israel is attacked by Arab neighbors on the south, west, and north: Egypt, Jordan, and Syria. In addition, Iraq, Saudi Arabia, Kuwait, and Algeria sent troops and assistance to attack Israel. In only six days, vastly outnumbered Israel miraculously

regained East Jerusalem from Jordan, the Golan Heights from Syria, and Sinai and Gaza from Egypt.[9]

- Yom Kippur War (October 1973)—Egypt and Syria intentionally launch a surprise attack on the Jewish holiday of Yom Kippur in an attempt to regain the territories lost to the Israelis during the Six-Day War. Once again, Israel won.
- Palestinian aggression in South Lebanon (1971–1982)
- 1982 Lebanon War (1982)
- First Intifada (1987–1993)—A large Palestinian uprising in the West Bank (Samaria and Judea) and the Gaza Strip.
- Second Intifada (2000–2005)—Second Palestinian uprising, a period of intensified violence, which began in late September 2000.
- 2006 Lebanon War (summer 2006)
- Gaza War (December 2008–January 2009)
- Hamas rocket attacks on Israel (2014)—An IDF offensive after the kidnapping and murder of three Israeli teenagers, with continual attacks on Israel by Hamas militants, and discoveries of several dozen tunnels into Israel for the purposes of terrorizing and killing civilians.[10]

In between these wars and uprisings against Israel is a much longer list of continual skirmishes, resulting in the deaths of thousands of innocent Israeli civilians. One of our recent trips to Israel was sobering. We were taken to the Israel-Syria border where we were met with members of the Israeli Defense Forces. Pointing to some villages in the distance, our guide said, "That village is now controlled by Hezbollah, that one by al Nusra (a branch of al-Qaeda), the next one by al Nursa, the next one by the Syrian Army, the next one by al Nursa, then the next group of villages are controlled by some fifty different Jihad groups, and then down there, is ISIS." One half million Syrians have been killed, with millions more displaced.

Israel faces Hezbollah's estimated two hundred thousand sophisticated missiles from the north, massive chaos from northeast Syria, ISIS sympathizers moving into Jordon on the East, Egypt in the south, and Hamas, which has in its charter the destruction of the Jewish population, on the southwest. How would you like to live in such a community? No wonder Israel has to defend herself.

THE TWO-STATE SOLUTION

Some claim that if Israel just gave land to the Palestinians, referred to as the "two-state solution," then peace would prevail. The fact is that Israel has given up land and offered land repeatedly, but the Muslim Arabs continue to attack Israelis. Remember, Israel is tiny, only one-sixth of 1 percent of the Middle East. The remaining twenty-two Arab nations have 99.9 percent of the land. Israel is only eight million people surrounded by three hundred million Arabs, many of whom want them dead.

Even so, Israel has repeatedly offered land for peace. David Brog has outlined that process:

- Offer Number One—1937. The Peel Partition Plan. The British offered to divide Palestine into a Jewish State (20 percent) and an Arab State (70 percent) with 10 percent or so to be retained by Britain. The Zionists approved partition but asked for a larger percentage. The Arabs of Palestine and beyond completely rejected the idea of partition.[11]
- Offer Number Two—1947. The United Nations Partition Plan. The UN offered to divide Palestine 50/50 into

a Jewish State and an Arab State. The Jews said yes.
The Arabs rejected partition and launched a war to
destroy the Jewish state.[12]

- Offer Number Three—1967. Israel won the Six-Day
War and conquered the West Bank. Shortly thereafter,
the Israeli cabinet split between those who wanted to
return the West Bank to Jordan and those who wanted
to give it to the Palestinians. In September, the Arab
League issued its three no's: "No peace with Israel, no
recognition of Israel, no negotiations with it." That
ended the debate over the West Bank.[13]

- Offer Number Four—2000. At Camp David, Israeli
Prime Minister Ehud Barak offered Yasser Arafat all of
Gaza, Arab East Jerusalem and approximately 94 per-
cent of the West Bank with some land swaps from
Israel. Arafat said no. Shortly thereafter, the bloody
second intifada was launched and over a thousand
Israelis were killed in terror attacks.[14]

- Offer Number Five—2008. Israeli Prime Minister Ehud
Olmert offered Mahmoud Abbas all of Arab East Jerusalem and approximately 96 percent of the West Bank
with land swaps from Israel proper equal to the remaining 4 percent. Gaza had already been given to the Palestinians in 2005. Abbas asked for time to think about
the offer. He never got back to Olmert.[15]

The Palestinian Authority does not want *some* land. They want
all the land. With the Jews gone. You cannot negotiate with people
who want you dead.

For those who call for a two-state solution, understand that we
already have a two-state solution. In the forming of present day Israel,
Britain lopped off a stunning 75 percent of Israel's land mass to form

the State of Jordan in 1948.[16] The Jews accepted the remaining 25 percent of the land for themselves.[17] Arabs who do not desire to be with Jews can live in Jordan.

Furthermore, all the land that the Jews owned then was purchased. They paid for it. For decades they bought swamps and deserts. They rehabilitated the land. The same Arabs that sold it to them then wanted it back once they saw that it could be developed.

The Arabs who choose to live under Israeli authority have many rights and privileges. Arab Muslims serve in the Knesset.[18] Some even serve on the Supreme Court.[19] In fact, many Arabs living in the West Bank (Samaria and Judea) prefer Israeli control over the Palestinians.[20] Yet the demand for Israel's land never ends. If Israel were to give up total control of the West Bank, Israel would only be nine miles across at one point and unable to defend itself.

Israel is here to stay, something the enemies of Israel need to learn.

One of my favorite T-shirts is a list of the nations that have opposed Israel. What do they all have in common? These empires are gone. Why? If you bless Israel, you will be blessed. If you curse Israel, you will be cursed. If you don't like it, take it up with God.

CHAPTER TWENTY-SIX

THE ENVIRONMENT AND CLIMATE CHANGE

*As someone who lived under communism for most of my
life, I feel obliged to say that the biggest threat to freedom,
democracy, the market economy and prosperity at the
beginning of the 21st century is not communism or its
various softer variants. Communism was replaced by the
threat of ambitious environmentalism.*[1]

—VACLAV KLAUS, PRESIDENT OF THE CZECH REPUBLIC

*(Global warming) only enables the green crusaders to
declare at every opportunity that "everybody" believes
the global warming scenario, except for a scattered few
"deniers" who are likened to Holocaust deniers. The
difference is that we have the hardest and most painful
evidence that there was a Holocaust. But, for the global
warming scenario that is causing such hysteria, we have
only a movie made by a politician and mathematical models
whose results change drastically when you change a few of
the arbitrarily selected variables.*[2]

—THOMAS SOWELL

*In Europe, where climate change absolutism is at its
strongest, the quasi-religion of greenery in general and the
climate change issue in particular have filled the vacuum of
organized religion with reasoned questioning of its mantras
regarded as a form of blasphemy.*[3]

—NIGEL LAWSON, FORMER CHANCELLOR OF THE EXCHEQUER OF UK

T he *Washington Post* reported in 2006 that Al Gore "believes humans may have only ten years left to save the planet from turning into a total frying pan."[4] In his film *An Inconvenient Truth*, he predicted that the earth would be in a "true planetary emergency" unless greenhouse gasses were dramatically reduced.[5]

Here we are, more than ten years later. Was Al Gore right? Are we in "a total frying pan?" Are we in a "true planetary emergency" right now? Short answer: no. Al Gore did become very wealthy by making these false prophecies.[6]

I am neither a scientist nor the son of a scientist. Therefore, I am in the same condition as 99.9 percent of non-scientist Americans. I have to decide whom to believe and whom to question. All of us view life through the lenses of people we trust.

My own experience was shaped by an extended church-building program that lasted almost three long decades. Fighting us every step of the way were environmentalists of every type. At first, I naively thought we could work together. After all, they were for clean water, clean air and clean land. So was I.

But they revealed their *modus operandi* in one candid conversation in which they demanded an expensive traffic study. I asked, "If the report concludes that we will negatively impact the environment, how will you respond?" The leader of the environmental group said, "Then I will accept the study," meaning he would block our plans. "But," I asked, "what if the traffic study comes back positive, showing that our building will have no negative impact?" Without a moment's hesitation, he replied, "Then I will reject the study." In other words, he had already made up his mind to oppose our project, regardless of science and reason.

THE HEART OF THE ISSUE: THE WAY WE DO GOVERNMENT

Hardcore environmentalists see the earth as sacred unto itself, with human activity spoiling what should exist in its own benign state. For these activists, the government is a powerful tool for crushing any opposition to their vision. All of this became clear after listening to a speech by Don Hodel, U.S. secretary of energy (1982–1985), and secretary of the interior (1985–1989) under President Reagan. When discussing the chokehold radical environmentalists had placed on Americans, he noted that they had, in reality, little interest in clean water, clean air, and clean land. Rather, he said that *they want to change the way we do government.*

At the core, radical environmentalism is about control over you and, especially your land. It is socialism. But in reality, the earth is not ours. It is the Lord's, as Psalms 24:1 (KJV) so eloquently states: "The earth is the Lord's and the fullness thereof, the world and they that dwell therein." But until the Lord returns to restore all things for His glory (Revelation 21), we have temporary use of it. As stewards of the earth (Genesis 1:26), we are to wisely guard over what we temporarily own.

But certain self-appointed watchdogs think they know better than you, the land owner, how to be a good steward. Their environmental oligarchy asserts control through government-imposed laws, regulations, and media complicit mischaracterizations, leaving you with few options for the use and development of your privately-owned land. The bottom line is that they do not see the land as *yours.* They see it as *theirs* to protect, since *they* know what is best for "mother earth." Sheer government power, not reason, or objective data, or biblical truth, or popular vote, or even reality becomes the vehicle to control, limit, and ultimately remove our human footprint. This type of control requires no less than the conversion of our capitalist system into a full-throated, elitist-run, socialist state that owns and manages everything.

POLITICIZATION

Is the world actually warming, and is it threatening humans and the environment? Unfortunately, the politicization of global warming has overshadowed the science and left many people ignorant of the unbiased facts. Instead of approaching this important issue from an informed, objective, scientific perspective, many associate their climate belief with their party affiliation.

To fully understand the global warming issue, we first need to realize that at its core global warming is a battle between two worldviews in direct opposition: biblical truth and evolutionary untruths.

- Evolution dictates that the earth was somehow formed billions of years ago and our climate, animals, and humans have evolved over time.
- Creationism believes God created the earth in six days and rested on the seventh (Genesis 1:1–2:3). He created land and sea, plants and animals, man and woman to subdue, work and keep the earth (Genesis 2:15), and He continues to sustain the world for His purposes (Hebrews 1:3).

This biblical worldview framework is often trapped inside the walls of our churches when we lack the capacity to articulate sound science coupled with Scripture—resulting in Christians' utter befuddlement when addressing global warming.

CREATION CARE

Caring for our environment is important to every follower of Christ, because God has entrusted it to our care. Psalms 115:16 (ESV) says, "The heavens are the Lord's heavens, but the earth he has given to the children of man." Creation care is biblical. We are God's stewards of the world He has given to us. We have been instructed to subdue the earth and rule over it, meaning we are to be responsible for it. Genesis 1:28 reads, "God blessed them and said to them, 'Be fruitful and increase in number; fill the earth and subdue it. Rule over the fish in the sea and the birds in the sky and over every living creature that moves on the ground.'"

Yet God holds the world in His hands and in His power. It is not ours. We are stewards of it. A steward is one who oversees something, cares for something that is not his. Therefore, care of the planet is important to us all. Yet at the same time, people's lives are more important than the environment in which we live. Animals, birds, insects, plants, sea life, even the earth itself only reflect God's character and serve to teach us about the almighty Creator (Psalms 19; Job 12:7–10). In fact, Romans 1:20 tells us that the creation exists to display God's "invisible qualities—his eternal power and divine nature...clearly seen" so that we are all without excuse and must acknowledge the Lord that made all things. Human life is obviously very important to God, and only human life is eternal (John 3:16). This present earth and the environment will eventually come to an end (Revelation 21:1) as a new earth is in the making. Does this mean we can ignore the environment and our impact upon it? Of course not. There is, however, no moral equivalence between human life and the rest of creation.

IS GLOBAL WARMING REAL?

Despite Al Gore and President Obama's adamant claims that our environment is on the brink of disaster, there are actually vast amounts of conflicting evidence on the subject. According to the Global Warming Policy Foundation report in 2013, all the major global temperature datasets reveal the earth hasn't warmed since 1997.[7] In fact, not only has it not warmed, but NASA scientists are now discovering record levels of ice in the Arctic.[8]

The reason why evidence seems conflicting is that climate gauges are not always accurate. In addition, the science used to create this hyper-concern about global warming is based primarily on scientific models used to *predict* the rate at which the climate was *thought* to be changing. These models focused primarily on human generation of greenhouse gases and carbon emissions. While providing insight, the models never provided conclusive evidence of an impending, cataclysmic event caused by global warming

According to the World Climate Report, *Science Magazine* writer Richard Kerr stated, "Climate modelers have been 'cheating' for so long it's almost become respectable." And former NASA scientist, Dr. Roy Spencer, says climate models used by government agencies, "have failed miserably." Dr. Spencer actually analyzed ninety climate models against surface temperature and satellite temperature data and discovered over 95 percent of the models "have over-forecasted the warming trend since 1979."[9]

HUMAN GREENHOUSE GASES AND CO2 EMISSIONS

Prominent modern scientists are suggesting that the global warming that appeared to be happening for a couple of decades leading up through the 1990s was not actually caused by human generated carbon emission and greenhouse gases. Some facts you should know:

- An overwhelming 64 percent of geoscientists and engineers believe that humans are not creating a global warming crisis and global warming does not pose a serious problem.[10]
- Over 31,000 scientists have signed a petition saying humans do *not* cause global warming.[11]
- Over 400 prominent scientists disputed man-made global warming claims in 2007 in front of the U.S. Senate.[12]

Larry Vardiman, Ph.D, in his scholarly article "Does Carbon Dioxide Drive Global Warming?" stated, "The recent warming trend since about 1850 appears to be the continuation of the warming following the Little Ice Age, rather than a sudden upsurge after a long period of relatively uniform temperatures."[13] Vardiman goes on to say, "The detailed temperature record since 1850 shows a temperature decline between 1940 and 1970, which flies in the face of the explanation that a continuous exponential increase in carbon dioxide causes global warming. And the simultaneous record of temperature and carbon dioxide concentration in ice cores indicates that carbon dioxide concentration changes after temperature changes, not before, indicating that carbon dioxide is the result, not the cause, of global warming."[14]

The reality is this: we're all just fine. God remains in complete control of His creation. He has destroyed His creation and restored it (Genesis 7–9). He has controlled the weather—lightning, rain, hail and snow (Job 28:26, 37:3, 6; Job 38:22; Psalms 147:17; Haggai 2:17; Psalms 147:8, 16). And at the epicenter of this issue is the very existence of God himself. Paul summed it up in Romans 1:25, referring to those who "worshiped and served created things rather than the Creator—who is forever praised." One must worship either the Creator or the creation. The choice is yours.

I choose the Creator.

ISLAM AND TERRORISM

But certainly, we know that there is a small group, and we don't know how big that is—it can be anywhere between five and twenty percent—that Islam is their religion and who have a desire for a caliphate and to institute that in any way possible.... They are willing to use and they do use terrorism.[1]

—DEMOCRATIC REPRESENTATIVE LORETTA SANCHEZ ON *POLITICKING WITH LARRY KING*

Some will object to Islam and terrorism being in the same chapter title together. But facts are such stubborn things. As of this writing there have been at least 28,348 deadly Islamic terrorist attacks worldwide since 9-11.[2] Four hundred fifty out of 452 suicide terrorist acts have been Islamic. At least 95 percent of all on-going wars and violence have roots in Islam.[3]

Some might exclaim, *there are more peaceful Muslims than there are radical Muslims.* This is true. We all know that. Like most of you, I have friends who are Muslims, and I value their relationships, most notable was my late wife's oncologist, who became an extremely close family friend. On May 16, 2016, I had the privilege of speaking at the United Nations at a special conference on creating a "family friendly world," and many of the twenty-six sponsoring member nations are Muslim nations. But that is beside the point. The focus of this chapter is not on the majority of Muslims that are peaceful. If only 15 percent are radicalized—as some contend—a staggering number of global killers are still on the loose. Every single day, innocent people are being raped, burned, tortured, beheaded, and killed in the name of the alleged "religion of peace" founded by Muhammad.

HISTORY OF ISLAM

Why are Muslims engaging in this violence? Why not Christians, Jews, Hindus, Buddhists, Sikhs, Taoists, or Chinese Folk Religionists? Why is this one particular religious—*and political*—structure causing such chaos? The history of Islam explains it all.

Muhammad, the father of Islam, was born in AD 570 in Mecca, in modern Saudi Arabia. He grew up in the Quraysh tribe, which embraced polytheism.[4] Around AD 610, Muhammad claimed he received his first vision from the Allah's Archangel Gabriel.[5] For twelve years Muhammad claimed he received visions from Allah, causing him to embrace monotheism.

Muhammad believed he was the last prophet sent from God. He believed he was sharing the same faith of Adam, Abraham, Moses and the "prophet" Jesus. Muhammad declared to the people in Mecca that he was Allah's final prophet; however, few believed him and still fewer followed him.[6] He later moved to the city of Medina where he built his mosque. It was there that much of the Muslim expansion began. Muhammad believed it was his duty to enforce Islam on others.[7] If people did not convert, they were killed. This has continued to the present. Before a nation adheres to Islam it is called a Dar-ul-Hard or *battlefield*; after a nation is converted, it is called Dar-us-Salaam or a *land of peace*.[8]

Muslims have five main beliefs:

1. Allah is the one true God.
2. Angels are instruments of God's, specifically bringing the words of the Qur'an to Muhammad.
3. The Qur'an is an infallible book.
4. There are many prophets (including Moses and Jesus), but Muhammad is the last prophet.
5. Everyone will be judged by Allah. Paradise and hell await the blessed and the damned respectively.[9]

Note: there is no separation of church and state in Islam. They are combined into a theocracy. Islam is a system that uses military power, political influence, legal authority, and the regulation of culture itself.

Many wrongly compare Islam to Christianity by pointing out the violence in the Old Testament. That comparison only demonstrates an ignorance of the major message of the Old Testament. When Joshua uses the sword as he entered the Promised Land, the alleged ethnic cleansing was limited to a very small geographical area comprised of Hittites, Amorites, Canaanites, Perizzites, Hivites and Jebusites (Deuteronomy 20:16–18). It occurred (1) because of the incredible wickedness of the nations that were occupying the land (Deuteronomy 18:9–14) and (2) because God had made a promise to the Patriarchs to give their offspring the land and He kept that promise (Genesis 12:5–7). Moses wrote: "It is not because of your righteousness or your integrity that you are going in to take possession of their land; but on account of the wickedness of these nations, the Lord your God will drive them out before you, to accomplish what he swore to your fathers, to Abraham, Isaac and Jacob" (Deuteronomy 9:5).

In addition, it happened for a very short period of time, as the Israelites entered Canaan, in contrast to Islam's constant jihad. Finally, it was for a very specific reason, that is, to keep the Israelites separate (distinct) from all other pagan nations. In the Old Testament the recurring theme is for Israel's *separation*, so God would have time to pour His truth into Israel for them to understand Yahweh (God) and His ways, and to have a people that were holy (Leviticus 20:26) as the Lord dwelt amongst them (Exodus 29:45).

In contrast to the Old Testament's call for separation in preparation for the coming Messiah (Jesus Christ) (Galatians 4:4–5), the New Testament calls for going into all the world. (Matthew 28:19) Furthermore, in the New Testament church, the sword is never used to advance the Gospel (Matthew 26:52) but only for self-defense (Luke 22:35–38). This is far different from Islam's belief of evangelizing by violence and death that has continued to this day with their doctrine remaining unchanged from the time of Muhammad.

THE TENETS OF ISLAMIC PRACTICE

Islam is the second largest religion in the world, behind Christianity, with over 1.6 billion adherents, representing 23 percent of the global population.[10] Despite being the second largest and the fastest growing world religion, according to Pew Research, Islam is one of the most misunderstood religions. It is misunderstood particularly because Western political correctness has distracted us from understanding the tenets of Islam. Our societal and cultural desire to accept everyone has stopped us from acknowledging the evil clearly written into Islamic tenets.

Muslims practice five key pillars:

1. The creed: "There is no God but Allah, and Muhammad is his messenger."
2. Daily prayers (Salat)
3. The fast of Ramadan
4. Almsgiving (Zakat)—giving 2.5 percent of their wealth away
5. The pilgrimage (Hajj) to Mecca[11]

Islam also has an *unofficial* sixth pillar: Jihad, which means *spiritual fight*. In my book *A Christian's Response to Islam*, I explained that spiritual fight can be "Jihad of the tongue: talking about Islam, Jihad of the hand: doing good works, Jihad of the heart: living the Islamic faith and lastly, Jihad of the sword: attacking others in the name of Allah." We know this final one as terrorism.[12]

Below are some quotes from the Quran, including the Sura (a chapter within the Quran), explaining Muslims' call to Jihad.

- Quran 9:5, "Then when the sacred months (the first, seventh, eleventh and twelfth months of the Islamic calendar) have passed, then kill the Mushrikam (idolaters) wherever you find them, and capture them, and prepare for them each and every ambush."
- Al-Bukhari 1:25, "Muhammad was once asked: What is the best act for the Muslim next to believing in Allah and His Apostle? His answer was: 'to participate in Jihad in Allah's cause.'"
- Sura 5:51, "Believers, take neither Jews nor Christians for your friends. They are friends with one another. Whoever of you seeks their friendship will become one of their number. Allah does not guide wrongdoers."
- Sura 9:29, "Fight against such of those to whom the scriptures were given as believe neither in Allah nor the last day, who do not forbid what Allah and His apostle have forbidden and do not embrace the true faith until they pay tribute out of hand and are utterly subdued."
- Sura 3:85, "If any one desires a religion other than Islam, never will it be accepted of him."
- Sura 3:157, "And if you are slain, or die in the way of Allah, forgiveness and mercy from Allah are far better than all they could amass."

- Al-Bukhari 9:64, "Allah's Apostle said, 'During the last days there will appear some young foolish people who will say the best words but their faith will not go beyond their throats and will go out from their religion as an arrow goes out of the game. So, whenever you find them, kill them, for whoever kills them shall have reward on the Day of Resurrection.'"[13]

THE CALIPHATE

The Caliphate was the Islamic government following Muhammad's death. *Caliph* means successor, and prior to Muhammad's death a successor was not named. Division and conflict pressured the Islamic faith to resolve who would become the successor and govern the caliphate. Some believed the successor should be Ali, Muhammad's son-in-law. This group became known as Shias, while another group believed those who worked closest with Muhammad should lead. They became the Sunnis. Sunnis dominated the religion for over five hundred years. They governed an empire that spanned portions of three continents, from Baghdad to Istanbul, until 1924 when World War I ended the Caliphate.[14]

Muslims have long desired to reestablish their world rule. Just four years later in 1928, The Muslim Brotherhood formed in Egypt as the first official effort to re-establish Islamic rule. Most recently in 2014, ISIS, the Islamic State in Iraq and Syria, announced a new Islamic Caliphate. ISIS has taken over much of Syria and Iraq, slaughtering tens of thousands of Christians and anyone who fails to comply with Islamic law.[15]

Islamic law has a track record of being among the most oppressive governments in the world. Twenty-two countries make up the League of Arab Nations.[16] Approximately forty nations have a Muslim majority.[17]

These countries, even those diplomatic with the U.S., are often violators of human rights. For example, Saudi-Arabia has diplomatic ties with the U.S., but is one of the worst violators of human rights, specifically in their persecution of Christians.[18] According to the Human Rights Watch, Saudi-Arabia also continued to restrict basic freedoms in 2015 such as due process and trial rights, freedom of expression and policies discriminating against women.[19]

IS ISLAMIC TERRORISM GROWING?

We are all likely aware of the following attacks:

- 2001—the attacks of 9/11
- 2009—mass shooting at Fort Hood Military Base by Islamist Nidal Hassan
- 2013—Boston Marathon Bombing
- 2015—series of terrorist attacks in Paris
- The rise of ISIS in the Middle East and Christian persecution in Iraq and Syria
- 2015—San Bernardino mass shooting terrorist attack
- 2016—deadly attacks in Belgium

But we only hear about the most visible attacks. Before, during, and after each of them were hundreds of smaller-scale, deadly attacks—a staggering 28,348.[20] We need to declare a war on Islamic terrorism for our own safety, the safety of our allies, and the safety of Christians around the world. The politicians we elect should lead the way by allowing our military to do their job—to locate and kill those who would use mass terror for global power and religious domination. Politically correct—read *dishonest*—politicians who ignore the facts only aid the slaughter of innocents.

RESPONDING AS CHRISTIANS

First, do not be intimidated to label evil what it is. The Scriptures warn: "Woe to those who call evil good and good evil." (Isaiah 5:20).

Second, we are to firmly and accurately speak the truth in love (Ephesians 4:15). We must expose the tenets of Islam for the evil it is, so it cannot be ignored by the politically misguided (Ephesians 5:11).

Third, care about those who are deceived. There are 1.6 billion Muslims worldwide who need to know of Christ's love. Some of them likely live in your neighborhood. Do not shy away from them. Form meaningful relationships. Do not hesitate to share truth. Become informed on how to share the message of Christ Jesus in a winsome and loving way, just as Paul became all things to all people to share the gospel (1 Corinthians 9:19–23) without compromising the truth. Truth and love are not mutually exclusive. Let us be a church that exercises both (John 3:16; Matthew 22:39).

Fourth, speak up. Let your elected officials know that political correctness is dishonest, shortsighted, and overlooks human suffering at the hands of Islamic terrorism. Ignoring or minimizing this evil will only give it strength and make it even more difficult to confront in the future.

Finally, pray and fast for our world. Some things come only by prayer and fasting (Mark 9:29, KJV) as we prayerfully seek the Lord's will and prepare for the days ahead (Ephesians 6:10–19).

CHAPTER TWENTY-EIGHT

REFUGEES

*Give me your tired, your poor, your huddled masses
yearning to breathe free, the wretched refuse of your
teeming shore. Send these, the homeless, tempest-tossed, to
me: I lift my lamp beside the golden door.*[1]

—EMMA LAZARUS

The Statue of Liberty has stood as a symbol of welcome to the world's outcast and refugees. For one hundred and thirty years, American immigrants have been greeted by this symbol of liberty as their ships sailed into the New York harbor or their flight landed.

A refugee is a person who has been forced to leave his country in order to escape war, persecution, or natural disaster. A refugee is not an immigrant or one who crosses a border for purposes of employment.

The world's refugee crisis is steadily growing. According to the United Nations there are over sixty million refugees and internally displaced people (IDP). That means for every 122 people in the world there is one refugee.[2]

Our current refugee crisis is being caused by turmoil in the Middle East. More than 9.5 million Syrians, almost half of the country's population, have been displaced.[3] One third of the world's refugees come from Iraq and Syria.[4] But the refugee crisis caused by radical Islam is spreading into other countries, as well.

On March 14, 2016, the U.S. House of Representatives resolved unanimously that the Islamic State's assaults on religious minorities in Iraq and Syria constitute genocide, a rare designation advocates hope will draw attention to the plight of persecuted groups.[5] Unanimous votes are extremely rare. Even backers of the bill were surprised. But such horrific refugee suffering moved everyone.

Calling it genocide cannot undo the extensive death and destruction, but it does appropriately honor those who were killed and focuses attention on aid for those who have survived.

PERSONAL STORY 1: CHALDEANS

I live in a suburb of San Diego, California, called El Cajon. More than 80,000 Chaldeans live in our community. They are not Muslims. They are Iraqi Christians. During the rapid movement of ISIS, we became aware of the anguish of many Iraqi Chaldeans through our Chaldean neighbors. I reached out to the local Bishop of the Chaldean Catholic Church and to a young Chaldean leader in our community to come speak to our congregation.

Their brief interview turned into a twenty minute Holy Spirit moment. Our congregation sat silent as the Bishop explained the atrocities. The young Chaldean man who followed him was equally spellbinding. He had collected the names of 80,000 of their friends, relatives, and acquaintances in Iraq who were in desperate need of help before ISIS got to them.

Since the nearby St. Peter Chaldean Catholic Church was fundraising for these refugees that next week, I encouraged our congregation to attend and support this worthy cause. At that event in the Catholic Chaldean Church I was asked to speak briefly. I asked, "How many here tonight are from my church?" About one-third of the large crowd raised their hands. Many of the Chaldean congregants audibly gasped. They were stunned to see that much love and support coming from a distinctly American, Protestant evangelical group.

As I closed my remarks, I recalled the famous speech by President John F. Kennedy in Berlin, Germany, June 26, 1963, in which he said in German, "I am a Berliner."[6] His words underscored the solidarity of America with the Berlin residents who were totally surrounded by Communists in East Germany. I closed my own remarks by saying, "Tonight, I am a Chaldean." They clapped and cheered. But I added, "President Kennedy made his statement of solidarity in Berlin in the German language. Allow me to attempt to do the same, only in Chaldean." A Chaldean man had helped me memorize the proper words. I repeated, "I am a Chaldean," but this time they heard it in their native language. They cheered. Some seemed to cry. Many hugged me afterward. They were so grateful that our congregation had expressed solidarity with them in this hour of deep pain. This was not merely symbolic on our parts. We felt and still feel the pain of their losses.

Our two congregations raised a lot of money for the refugees that night. But the next time I was with the young Chaldean leader who had the list of eighty thousand in harm's way, twelve thousand of them had been killed. Twelve thousand! I was stunned. *What could we have done?*

PERSONAL STORY 2: IN DEFENSE OF CHRISTIANS

My wife and I attended an event in Washington, D.C., put on by an organization known as "In Defense of Christians," composed of Catholics, Orthodox, and Anglicans from many Middle East nations. Only two evangelicals were involved in the opening night worship service: one from Lebanon and me.

I was the only Protestant American pastor. It is likely that most pastors did not know about the meeting, but it was heartbreaking to me that so many of our Christian brothers and sisters were being slaughtered in the Middle East while we seemed so oblivious. It is not that the major news outlets haven't painted a graphic picture of the barbaric torture, beheadings, rapes and destruction. It isn't that we have never been shocked by the violence occurring against those of faith. It is a heart issue that must move us to take action of some kind, any kind, instead of waiting for the inevitable. James 4:17 (ESV) is clear: "So whoever knows the right thing to do and fails to do it, for him it is sin." We know who needs help; we have resources; are we willing to use them?

LOVE YOUR NEIGHBOR AS YOURSELF

Matthew 25:34–36, 40, is a deeply moving passage on how Christians are to treat those in need:

> Come, you who are blessed by my Father; take your inheritance, the kingdom prepared for you since the creation of the world. For I was hungry and you gave me something to eat, I was thirsty and you gave me something to drink, I was a stranger and you invited me in, I needed clothes and you clothed me, I was sick and you looked after me, I was in prison and you came to visit me.... Whatever you did for one of the least of these brothers of mine, you did for me.

As Christians, we are to respond to refugees with Christ's compassion and wisdom. Yet Matthew 10:16 (RSV) cautions, "Be wise as serpents and innocent as doves." It is possible to be at once wise and compassionate—the two are not mutually exclusive. We are to balance compassion, wisdom and objective reality, recognizing that we are to seek the Lord's will in how we are to best minister to those that are suffering. Scripture gives us a promise in this regard. James 1:5 (ESV) says that in difficult times, "If any of you lacks wisdom, let him ask God, who gives generously to all without reproach, and it will be given him." We need this wisdom to govern our national response to the refugee crisis, our proper corporate church response, and even our own individual actions that we may be led to take.

MUSLIMS OR CHRISTIANS?

It is critical to distinguish between two radically different groups of refugees: Muslims and Christians. Over 96 percent of the Syrian refugees admitted into the United States in early 2016 have been Muslims. Only a little over 2 percent have been Christians.[7] Why is this so disproportionate? Because Christians have been driven from United Nations camps. They hide in private residences and churches. They are terrified to put their names on the UN lists because of further persecution, so they receive no aid. No one has come to the Christians' rescue.[8]

True ethnic cleansing is happening to Christians in the Middle East, yet they have received no preference for help by our nation. Neighboring Muslim countries can and should take in fellow Muslim refugees and provide them with aid and care. The U.S. should come to the aid of Christians, given the fact that they pose no present danger (terrorism) and have the greatest chance of assimilating into a nation with an overwhelming Christian environment and legacy. *There is no Muslim nation in the Middle East where Christians can go.* In fact, Israel is the only nation in which Christians are free in the Middle East.

Admittedly no "religious" test should prohibit a person—Christian or Muslim—from coming to the United States. However, given the fact that the director of the FBI has publically stated that the FBI has no files on the Muslims wanting to come in from nations with many terrorist groups, there should be—how do we say this?—a "violence" test or a "terrorism" test. This is not "racial" profiling. It is "terrorism" profiling. And that is right. After all, the role of the government is to protect its citizenry. The government of the United States needs to be able to discern who the people are who want to come in before they are allowed in.

While Americans have been kind, compassionate, and historically welcoming to the world's refugees—Americans don't need to hang their heads about this fact—they do have a legitimate right for incoming persons to be thoroughly vetted. U.S. citizens have a right to expect that their government can verify that the Muslims arriving on our shores from these terrorism-ridden nations are, in fact, authentically peaceful and affirming of American ways and values. If they are, they are welcome.

Americans have a right to be concerned about a disproportinate number of young, fighting-age males embedded among Muslim refugees. Any attempt to "guilt" people who raise such questions is inappropriate. In light of the recent San Bernardino and other killings, it is totally appropriate for Americans to insist that the current administration have precise and 100 percent accurate techniques to ferret out would-be terrorists before allowing Muslims to enter. That is not xenophobia. That is prudence.

At the same time, the Christian ministry opportunities toward the Muslims that are coming in are a remarkable opportunity for churches. Like many churches, our church strongly promotes and supports ministry among the arriving refugees, Christian or Muslim. For the Muslims who have never been exposed to the love of Christ and the Gospel of forgiveness, this is a spectacular moment for outreach and ministry.

Recognizing Christians' dire situation in the Middle East should cause our nation to respond with whatever means available to support their safe relocation—whether that place is the United States or with other western nations that have histories compatible with the roots of Christian refugees. Heed the warning of 1 John 3:17 (ESV), "But whoever has the world's goods, and sees his brother in need and closes his heart against him, how does the love of God abide in him?" This course of action acknowledges the security risks that come with certain groups, while reaching out to those with whom we have the closest compatibility, so that we are not merely looking out for our own personal interests, but also for the interests of others (Philippians 2:4).

PART VII

POLITICAL PARTICIPATION

MEDIA

The liberty of the press is essential to the security of freedom in a state: it ought not, therefore, to be restrained in this commonwealth.[1]

—JOHN ADAMS, SAMUEL ADAMS, JAMES BOWDOIN

When newspapers knock a man a lot, there is sure to be a lot of good in him.[2]

—WILL ROGERS

Freedom of the press is the legally protected freedom of expression and communication through print, media, electronic media and publishing, without the control or interference of the government. But what responsibility do members of the media have?

I admit it. I am a news junky. When I was a young child growing up on a farm in north central Kansas we were the second family in our entire farming area to have a TV.

I was immediately hooked on the news. As a seven-year-old, even *I Love Lucy* and *Davy Crockett* did not compare to watching the news.

My heroes were John Cameron Swayze, Douglas Edwards, Edward R. Murrow, Chet Huntley, and David Brinkley—to name a few.

I tell you this so you will know what admiration I have for the profession of journalism. After I finish an interview, I will occasionally tell the reporter how much I appreciate their professional calling. They generally react with surprise at my affirmation. But as much as I admire the profession, a full disclosure is in order.

THE THEOLOGICAL BASIS FOR THE MEDIA

The First Amendment guarantee of a free press is implicitly and *theologically* important. A free media exists for the same reason we have three branches of government. Each branch checks and balances the other—because of the capacity for evil in the human heart. Jeremiah 17:9 (ESV) summarizes it well: "The heart is deceitful above all things, and desperately sick; who can understand it?"

An objective media performs the incredibly important function of independently challenging power. This function aligns with Proverbs 18:17 (ESV), "The one who states his case first seems right, until the other comes and examines him." The balance only works, however, if the media is not in bed with the government or being intentionally antagonistic.

OBJECTIVITY AND COMPETENCE

One of the foundational values of journalism is objectivity. There was a day when news anchors were trusted. I remember the first time the news media disappointed me. My cousin, my brother, and his college roommate all died in a plane crash. The sloppy newspaper reporters did not even get the victim's ages correct. I remember wondering why they could not have done a more thorough job.

A few years later, I was at a pro-life event in front of an abortion center. There were approximately three hundred pro-lifers and twenty-five abortion advocates. The reporter positioned herself at a point of separation between our large group and their tiny group. As the cameras rolled, I was stunned to hear the reporter say, "As you can see, about the same numbers of persons showed up on each side of this issue." What! There were ten times as many pro-lifers there as pro-abortionists. But she had arranged the background so that only seven or eight could be seen on each side. As one who had idolized those in the media, the dishonesty was disillusioning.

Trying to be as objective as possible when reporting a crime, a political policy, or a tragic event is hard work. Our emotions can become entangled in the story—yet Scripture explains how we are to be objective. We should "not be partial to the poor or defer to the great, but in righteousness shall you judge your neighbor" (Leviticus 19:15, ESV). Can we honestly say this describes our media today?

DISTRUST

I am not alone in my distrust of at least some of the media. No wise person would perceive the media as truly objective today. Many news anchors are in the hip pocket of certain candidates who fit within their ideology and the established narrative.

Consider that nearly nine out of ten Americans strongly or somewhat agree that the media have their own political and public policy positions and attempt to influence public opinion.[3] The Pew Research Center reports that only 25 percent of poll respondents think reporters consistently get the facts correct,[4] and only 18 percent said the media reports the news fairly.[5] The lack of professionalism and honesty demonstrated by modern journalists—a profession traditionally so respected—is an enormous loss for our nation.

Being in the public eye, speaking about important events or reporting on an influential person is exhilarating and demanding. Journalists and news reporters occupy positions of incredible influence, and the temptation can be both subtle and self-serving to spin a story to promote personal views. But as the public opinion polls show, "bread gained by deceit is sweet to a man, but afterward his mouth will be full of gravel" (Proverbs 20:17, ESV). When deceit takes the guise of objectivity, bias turns into dishonesty.

Why have members of this honorable profession lost credibility? They are biased. Bias is not, in itself, a sin. Bias is human. But denying one's bias is delusional at best and dishonest at worst.

Can the media regain our trust? Possibly. Possibly not. I write this as one who is a fan of the media, who really admires the professional calling of journalism. That said, I propose a method for regaining the trust that news reporters—primarily *political* reporters—have lost.

ADMIT THE OBVIOUS

The first step is to admit that complete objectivity is not possible. Carey Morewedge of Boston University's Questrom School of Business expressed it perfectly: "It is believed by the social sciences that all people have bias—and a 'bias blind spot,' meaning that they are less likely to detect bias in themselves than others.... People seem to have no idea how biased they are. Whether a good decision-maker or a bad one, everyone thinks that they are less biased than their peers. This susceptibility to the bias blind spot appears to be pervasive, and is unrelated to people's intelligence, self-esteem, and actual ability to make unbiased judgments and decisions."[6] Blind spots affect us all, but most of us do not claim absolute objectivity. However, most media outlets and their on-air personalities do.

The second step is for journalists to have a "bias report," a non-objectivity acknowledgement. Every journalist who reports on political matters would have to indicate publically for whom and for what political party they have voted in the past four presidential cycles.

If someone appears to be slanted in their reporting, a viewer or reader can check how that journalist voted in the past. I merely ask the media to practice the same full disclosure they demand of the government. If the media view themselves as the ones keeping the government honest, then who is going to keep the media honest? Some reporters might call foul. But let's check the reality. Only 7 percent of journalist are registered as Republicans.[7] There is no party affiliation quota for journalists. But the innate bias is leading to mistrust of a vital component of a democracy: a free—*and honest*—media.

Even though the number of reporters who are registered Democrats has been dropping since polling began in 1971 and the number of journalists registered as Independents has increased,[8] the issue is not how members of the media are *registered* but—as it relates to bias—*how did they vote*. Reporter bias is not some new academic problem. It is an extended epidemic. It has been this way for decades:

- More than four-fifths of surveyed journalists said they voted for the Democratic presidential nominee in every election between 1964 and 1976.[9]
- In 1992, 88 percent of surveyed D.C. reporters said they voted for Bill Clinton for president.[10] In 2004, the same group said it supported Democrat John Kerry over President George W. Bush by a 12-to-1 margin.[11]
- In 2009, a whopping 96 percent of the staff working for the online Slate magazine said they supported Barack Obama for president.[12]

In the American Society of Newspaper Editors poll, when asked "how often do journalists' opinions influence coverage?" a solid majority of the editors (57 percent) conceded it "sometimes" happens while another 14 percent said opinions "often" influence news coverage. In contrast, only 1 percent claimed it "never" happens, and 26 percent said personal views "seldom" influence coverage.[13]

Am I too hard on the media? Not at all. I truly admire the profession. But I am asking for full disclosure out of a desire to restore the public's trust for reporters. Registering his or her voting record is a way of honestly acknowledging biases that will color the stories they are reporting. I am not calling for the government to be involved. I would hope that the profession would have the nobility to police itself.

CHAPTER THIRTY

NULLIFICATION AND CIVIL DISOBEDIENCE

Rebellion against tyrants is obedience to God.[1]

—BENJAMIN FRANKLIN'S GREAT SEAL DESIGN (FOR THE U.S.) AUGUST 1776

...A tyrannical "government" is not really a government at all but a criminal gang masquerading as a government, and is therefore not entitled to the obedience that governments (properly so called) can claim. The principle of the rule of law.... implies the right to rebellion.[2]

—GOVERNMENTAL THEORY SCHOLAR GREG FOSTER

The Founders of our nation anticipated a strong government might be tempted to overreach its constitutional limitations. They were correct. The good news is they provided remedies.

As early as 1798, the U.S. Congress passed the Alien and Sedition Acts.[3] They contained penalties for criticizing certain parts of the government, clearly an entirely unconstitutional restriction and a threat to the First Amendment. Kentucky passed the famous 1798 Kentucky Resolutions, written by Thomas Jefferson.[4] Kentucky resolved they would not recognize the validity of the Acts in Kentucky. Other states soon followed.

This is the spirit of the Tenth Amendment to the Constitution. It says, "The powers not delegated to the United States by the Constitution, nor prohibited by it to the States, are reserved to the States respectively, or to the people."[5]

The federal government was created by the States and is subject to them. The States retain all rights and powers except for the thirty explicitly delegated to the federal government and enumerated in the Constitution.[6]

In 1850, Congress passed the Fugitive Slave Act. It required those in free northern states to return fleeing slaves to southern slaveholders. Wisconsin and other northern states refused to recognize the validity of the Act. They deemed the Supreme Court opinion that denied the full personhood of slaves to be unconstitutional.[7]

Ignoring and defying unconstitutional federal law is called nullification. When the federal government acts outside of its enumerated powers, it has exercised an illegitimate authority, a ruling not to be respected.

Nullification is gaining prominence as a way to reverse two of the most egregious Supreme Court decisions in the last fifty years: *Roe v. Wade* denied the humanity and personhood of the baby in the womb and decriminalized abortion. The *Obergefell* opinion created a right to same-sex "marriage." Both rulings were based on the political, ideological agendas of a handful of unelected justices. No rights to abortion or same-sex "marriage" can be found in the Constitution.

States retain to this day the right to nullify unconstitutional opinions and laws. We need principled, *constitutional,* pro-life, and pro-family state legislators and governors to defy the Feds and enforce state laws.

CITIZEN NULLIFICATION

But nullification doesn't stop at the state level. A strong precedent is growing for local citizens to nullify ungodly (and unjust) laws. The latter part of the Tenth Amendment implies that if a federal law is unconstitutional, or state law is ungodly or offensive, then citizens have the power to ignore them. This claim actually has some biblical merit. In 1 Samuel 14:1–45 while King Saul was pursuing the Philistines, he vowed death to anyone who ate anything before sundown. His son, Jonathan, unaware of the king's edict, ate some honey. The men around him did not allow Jonathan to be executed for violating his father's oath since he had not known and he had been the hero of a great victory that day. The rash oath of the king was nullified by his own fighting men.

In our own country, after passage in 1850 of the Fugitive Slave Law, northern jurors refused to convict abolitionists who violated the law and refused to return runaway slaves to their masters in slave states. The law was unjust, and it could not be enforced because citizens refused to respect it—that was nullification. Samuel Chase, U.S. Supreme Court justice and signer of the Declaration of Independence said in 1796: "The jury has the right to determine both the law and the facts."[8] And Harlan F. Stone, the chief justice of the Supreme Court said in 1941: "The law itself is on trial quite as much as the cause which is to be decided."[9] There are numerous examples of nullification over the years, and they highlight a key justice principle—a jury is responsible to deliver justice, not to blindly uphold an unjust law.

These are powerful responsibilities for an individual to exercise, and they should not be taken lightly. When a law violates the authority entrusted into the hands of our representative government, if it violates God's righteous laws intended for our good and not harm, and if it causes us to violate our own conscience, then we must be willing to *nullify* that law in godly ways. If necessary, we must be prepared to suffer the consequences that may come to us as a result and entrust ourselves to a merciful God.

However, citizen nullification is not an excuse for wanton disregard for law. If you don't agree with the speeding limit, you still can't speed. Citizen nullification should be based on strict constitutionality and our laws' Judeo-Christian underpinnings. Make these decisions cautiously and with healthy respect for civil government.

Martin Luther King Jr. wrote "One may well ask: How can you advocate breaking some laws and obeying others? The answer lies in the fact that there are two types of laws: just and unjust. I would be the first to advocate obeying just laws. One has not only a legal but a moral responsibility to obey just laws. Conversely, one has a moral responsibility to disobey unjust laws. I would agree with St. Augustine that 'an unjust law is no law at all.'"[10]

CIVIL DISOBEDIENCE

I was in a meeting in New York City a few years ago with a group of eighty biblically-attuned, theologically-sophisticated, and politically-astute activists. We were discussing the rapid evaporation of religious liberty. One older gentleman in a suit and tie stood and surprised us with a question, "At what point are we pressed to the point of civil disobedience?" We were quiet. He had courageously addressed the elephant in the room. We all realized that standing for truth could cost us a lot more than we want to pay: openly disobeying the government. Simply because a law exists is not, in and of itself, a reason to obey it.

When this moment comes—and perhaps it has already—we will not be alone. Many have gone before us:

- The Egyptian midwives (Exodus 1:17, 21)
- Rahab (Joshua 2)
- Obadiah hiding God's prophets (1 Kings 18)
- Shadrach, Meshach, and Abednego (Daniel 3:13–27)
- Daniel (Daniel 6:13)
- Esther (Esther 4:16)

- The Magi (Matthew 2:8, 12)
- Peter and John (Acts 4:19–20, 5:29)
- Moses leading the Jews from Egyptian captivity (Exodus 14)

My Ph.D. is in Church history, and over the years I have given a talk entitled "The Church Alive and Well," a one-hour sweep through two thousand years of Christian history. The story is one of encouragement and the unstoppable nature of the Gospel. But it also contains many accounts of Christians having to defy both governmental and ecclesiastical authorities. That civil disobedience often cost them their lives. I will only recount a few here.

You are reading this page now because you are able to read English. For printing the Bible in English for the first time, William Tyndale, was choked to death in 1536, his body burned on the spot.[11] As he was being choked, his last words were, "Lord, open the King of England's eyes."[12] Two years later, the king changed his mind and started printing Tyndale's English Bible version in 1538.[13]

Another classic example of civil disobedience is Sir Thomas More, who defied Henry VIII as a matter of conscience and paid with his life in 1535. Yet Sir Thomas More was voted Lawyer of the Millennium by the secular British Legal Society in 2000 over such luminaries as Blackstone, Gandhi and many other worthy candidates.[14] The heroic civil disobedience of such martyrs has proven to be on the right side of history. Their sacrifices, like the sacrifices we may all be called to make soon, will also be on *the right side of eternity.*

Attorney Mat Staver is encouraging Christians not to allow the government to force them to violate their Christian convictions. His group vows at defendmarriage.org that "We will view any decision by the Supreme Court or any court the same way history views the *Dred Scott* and *Buck v. Bell* decisions. Our highest respect for the rule of law requires that we not respect an unjust law that directly conflicts with higher law...We respectfully warn the Supreme Court not to cross this line. While there are many things we can endure, redefining marriage is so fundamental to the natural order and the common good that this is the line we must draw and one we cannot and will not cross."[15]

The Manhattan Declaration, which has been signed by hundreds of thousands of serious followers of Jesus, closes with these words, "As Orthodox, Catholic, and Evangelical Christians, we take seriously the Biblical admonition to respect and obey those in authority. Because we honor justice and the common good, we will fully and ungrudgingly render to Caesar what is Caesar's. But under no circumstances will we render to Caesar what is God's."[16] May we have the discernment and courage to do what is right and obey God rather than man (Acts 4:19–20, 5:29).

CONCLUSION

NOW YOU KNOW WHAT TO SAY

CHAPTER THIRTY-ONE

A CALL TO ACTION AND THE REASON FOR HOPE

All the answers are in there.[1]

—MARCO RUBIO (REGARDING THE BIBLE)

We should always approach the interpretation and application of Scripture with a sense of profound humility. That said, I pray, "Lord, that I have been faithful to Your Word. But I have blind spots and limited understanding. In those areas where I have not understood the issues at hand, protect the reader from the errors of my writing. Where I have properly captured Your intent, burn that truth on their hearts. Where I have written or explained too little, I ask Your Holy Spirit to use my words as springboards that will take the readers' hearts and minds to that which You want them to see, far beyond what I know or am capable of writing. My desire is to honor You fully and to do justice to Your Holy Word. Amen."

THE CALL TO ACTION

The same Word of God that speaks to us, our families, and our churches, also speaks to our schools, workplaces, communities, and governments. There is no major world issue about which the Word does not provide basic and transcendent truths. Most people readily understand how biblical truths apply to their emotions, fears, desires, family life, and church life. But when we hear the word *political*, we shut our Bibles and recoil, as if God has no interest in government, in spite of the fact that it was God who first invented it (Isaiah 9:6). Christians—particularly pastors—seem to run from the political. The Evil One delights over this situation. But a Sovereign King refuses to yield any ground to the Evil One. He intends for us to do the same.

My call is not to political action, although political action is a very good thing. I am calling you to something much more stimulating and thrilling. I am calling you to biblical applicationalism. (If this word didn't exist before, it does now.) As followers of Jesus, we need to know how to apply the immeasurable principles of Scripture to—not 50 percent, 75 percent, or even 99 percent of life—but *every* issue of life. Yes, even politics. Given the disastrous condition of our government and those around the globe, I pray for a governmental anointing to come upon you right now, by the power of the Holy Spirit.

Study the Word for its governmental principles. Study this book and others like it. Equip yourself. Be disciplined. Enter into discussions. First with believers. And then with unbelievers. You—as one who will know the Word of God—will have the upper hand. Be loving, gracious, and winsome. But be bold and firm, as well. If you get beaten back for lack of understanding, regroup, study, and get back into the arena of ideas. Your ideas are superior not because they are yours, but because they are not yours. They are God's. His ways are best. Always.

If enough people came to know the Word of God as it relates to the government, then a highly informed, articulate electorate would elect people worthy of leading us. The results would be transformational to our nation. Individuals would be changed. Families would be restored. Churches would be energized. Schools and factories would be enhanced. Communities would be invigorated. Cities would be healed. States would be enlivened. Our nation would be restored. Our entire world would be changed.

I care not about your eschatology, or doctrine of end times. On this truth we can all agree: Jesus is Lord. His Word is good. It is to be proclaimed. That is my call to action.

THE REASON FOR HOPE

Jesus is the Son of God. Though He arrived in Bethlehem two thousand years ago, He preexisted. He always existed as the second member of the Trinity—Father, Son, and Holy Spirit. He did not have to be created. He always *is*, present tense. He is *always*.

Although we did not see Him in human flesh till the Bethlehem manger, He did appear on earth numerous times in what are called *Christophanies*, or Christ appearances. Sometimes the reader does not immediately recognize Him because of ambiguity or euphemisms (phrases such as "angel of the Lord").

When Joshua encountered the imposing man with the sword drawn in Joshua 5:13–15, Joshua was understandably shaken. He was a successful general, the leader of about two million people. He was a man's man, not easily intimidated. Joshua asked a most practical question, "Are you for us or our enemies?"

"Neither," the intimidating figure responded. "I am the commander of the army of the Lord!" Translate that: "I did not come here to take sides. I came here to take over." Who was this one? The pre-incarnate Jesus.

A modern day paraphrase of that passage would read: "Lord, are You a Democrat or a Republican?" "Neither. I am in charge of everything, including political parties."

What does this mean?

- Does that mean this book is about a theocracy? No. We are in a constitutional republic and would like it to stay that way (or return to that).
- Does that mean I am a dominionist? No. The dominion I believe in is found in Genesis 1:26 where God gave to humanity dominion—stewardship—over *His* earth.
- Does that mean I want to force my views on others? No. I want the presentation of biblical truth to be so convicting and so compelling *that people want to embrace it.*
- Does it mean that I am trying to politically outmaneuver or outvote the opposition? No. I want the opposition to understand heart-felt truths that cause them to want to live for Jesus in every aspect of their lives, including the voting booth.
- Does it mean that I am pushing a particular eschatology? No. It simply means I believe that Jesus is King and I am part of His Kingdom.

Joshua was not the only one who encountered this pre-existent Jesus. Gideon came face to face with Him in Judges 6:21 and Gideon—also a skilled military leader—was so terrified that the Lord had to assure him that he was not going to die. Manoah in Judges 13:19–21 encountered The One as well. Flames shot out of the sacrifice he had brought, causing him to cry out, "We are doomed to die! We have seen God!"

Then Jesus arrived on earth, born of a woman "overshadowed" by God Himself! By age twelve, He was able to exceed the understanding of the Ph.D.'s gathered in the Temple. When He called rough, tough fishermen James and John—known as the "sons of thunder" due to their rowdy ways—they dropped their nets and followed Him. When He called the highly successful owners of a fishing company—Peter and Andrew—to dump nets, boats, and profits, they left it all and began following Him. What kind of a man is this? He is no wimp. He is no milquetoast. He is a man's man. He told brawny, leathered, outdoor workers to leave their operations and follow Him. And they did!

Then came the miracles. First, He controlled time. He stopped it, reversed it, and elongated it, performing miracles of healing and even resurrection of the dead. Then he altered molecules and atoms. He fed 5,000 people from a dinky lunch of five slices of bread and a couple fish sticks. Water became wine and then Jesus walked on water.

Then came the Transfiguration, when Moses, dead for 1,400 years, and Elijah, dead for seven hundred years, showed up! Peter, James, and John—strong guys, were terrified. They fell down on their faces (Matthew 17:6). Peter started babbling—not even knowing what he was saying (Luke 9:33). This is some Jesus!

Then came the Crucifixion. Do you know what He said about it? "No one takes [my life] from me, but I lay it down of my own accord. I have authority to lay it down and authority to take it up again. This command I received from my Father" (John 10:18). Even in His death, He literally took on Satan and defeated him—before the Resurrection (Colossian 2:14; Hebrews 2:14)!

What about the time between the Crucifixion and the Resurrection? Where was He? What did He do? Scholars disagree on how to interpret I Peter 3:18–19, but the Apostles Creed says "he descended into hell." Why go to hell? Because there is no place that He can't go, and no place that is not His! He went to hell as a victory lap. Abraham Kuyper was right: "There is not a square inch in the whole domain of our human existence over which Christ, who is Sovereign over all, does not cry: 'Mine!'"

And then came that explosion of power called the Resurrection that blew a massive stone right off the tomb and caused Rome's most elite military guard to fall to the ground like dead men! (Matthew 28:4). What a God!

Then came appearances—to more than five hundred at one time—
and the Ascension in which He defied gravity and went up into the air.
The two angels who showed up to explain said, "This is the way he is
coming back."

Eventually the Rapture will come where we, the church, get to
feel the gravitational pull melt away ourselves. If you don't believe in
it, fine. I'll wave as I go up. And finally the second coming of Jesus
will come. He came the first time as a lamb and a servant. He will
return as a lion and a King. John, the close friend of Jesus, told us
what will happen. Hang onto to your seat as you read this passage
from Revelations 19:11–16:

> I saw heaven standing open and there before me was a white
> horse, whose rider is called Faithful and True. With justice
> he judges and makes war. His eyes are like blazing fire, and
> on his head are many crowns. He has a name written on
> him that no one knows but he himself. He is dressed in a
> robe dipped in blood, and his name is the Word of God.
> The armies of heaven were following him, riding on white
> horses and dressed in fine linen, white and clean. Out of his
> mouth comes a sharp sword with which to strike down the
> nations. "He will rule them with an iron scepter." He treads
> the winepress of the fury of the wrath of God Almighty. On
> his robe and on his thigh he has this name written: KING
> OF KINGS AND LORD OF LORDS.

A rider on a white horse. Eyes like blazing fire. Blood on His robe.
A sword coming out of His mouth. Armies riding behind Him. Ruling with an iron scepter. And His name? KING OF KINGS. All of
them. LORD OF LORDS. All of them!

We *will* stand before Him. A book *will* be opened. It will be the Book
of Life. If your name is in it, you will go to the *bema seat* where Christ
will be seated. A *bema* was a Greek term associated with competitions.

It was a raised platform where winning athletes got their prizes. Rewards will be handed out there for those covered by the righteousness of Christ. If your name is not in the Book of Life, you will go to the Great White Throne Judgment.

But that is not how it all ends. That is where it all begins for me—in eternity. I would like it to begin for you, too. In fact, I would like to spend forever with you.

Paul told us how to do that:

"For we will all stand before God's judgment seat. It is written: 'As surely as I live,' says the Lord, 'every knee will bow before me; every tongue will confess to God.' So then, each of us will give an account of himself to God" (Romans 14:10–12).

Every person will come to see that Jesus is God. For many it will be too late. I don't want you to be one of them. Right now, bow—either literally or figuratively—before him. And let your mouth reverently yet boldly say, "Jesus *is* Lord!"

ACKNOWLEDGMENTS

E very book is the result of a large team of people. This book is no exception to that fact.

Thank you to my wife Rosemary, my children, and grandchildren who were willing to allow me to be absent from so many family activities during a rather intense time of writing.

Thank you to the Skyline Church congregation, staff, and board who are so supportive of my efforts.

Thank you to Tracy Burger, the world's greatest administrative assistant, who manages my life so that I can do projects like this. She is remarkable.

Enormous contributions were made by a spectacular research and writing team who helped me write this book:

- Audrea Taylor—who brought the insights of a politically brilliant and culturally alert twenty-year-old
- Frank Kacer—a retired physicist who understands the application of biblical truth to political and social issues better than anyone I know
- Gary Cass—a pastor who "gets it," who has a staggering grasp of historical theology and its relevance to current culture

Without these three people, this book would not have happened. They met with me often. We prayed, processed, debated, struggled over concepts, and loved being with each other. What a team!

Thank you to Anne Subia who met with Audrea, Frank, and Gary repeatedly, helping to keep us focused.

Thank you to Bill Blankschaen who skillfully edited what I gave him. He was such a help throughout the process.

Thank you to Craig Osten who is a "fact checker" and "footnoter" extraordinaire. I marveled at his intellect and thoroughness.

Thank you to Alan Sears of ADF who graciously made Craig Osten available to me. What a gift!

Thank you so much to my colleagues at Regnery Publishing, beginning with the President Marji Ross and extending through the whole team. Working with them was a joy.

Thank you to Bob DeMoss who believed in me enough to be my "cheerleader" in the early phases of the proposal of the book. This started because of you.

Thank you to the "Scripture Checking Team" which consisted of: Jeanette Bell, Samantha Cole, Sonia Diaz, Bonnie Kane, Patti Kapaska, Todd Morgan, Greta Morgan, Donna Morrison, Raeburn Solberg, Eutha Scholl, Guy Smith, and Carla Washington.

I want to thank proofreaders Greta Morgan, Anne Subia, and my ninety-five-year-old mother Winifred Garlow who worked extended hours in an attempt to catch every detail under a crushing deadline.

I am grateful to God for the privilege He has granted me to write this book.

This book is a joint effort by so many. I am deeply grateful to partner with you all.

NOTES

CHAPTER ONE: WHY ARE WE QUIET?

1. "God's People Want to Know," American Culture and Faith Institute, September 24, 2015, http://www.culturefaith.com/gods-people-want-to-know/.
2. Michael Lipka, 5 Takeaways about Religion and Politics before the Midterms," Pew Research Center, September 22, 2014, http://www.pewresearch.org/fact-tank/2014/09/22/5-takeaways-about-religion-and-politics-before-the-midterms/.
3. "Public Sees Religion's Influence Waning," Pew Research Center, September 22, 2014, http://www.pewforum.org/2014/09/22/public-sees-religions-influence-waning-2/.

4.   Karla Dial, "Aiming for Goliath," *Citizen Magazine,* August 2008, p. 25.

5.   *Government Regulation of Political Speech by Religious and Other 501(c)(3) Organizations: A Report to Senator Charles Grassley with Recommendations for Congress and the Treasury Department* (Commission on Accountability and Policy for Religious Organizations, 2013): 14.

6.   Dial, "Aiming for Goliath," 26.

7.   Internal Revenue Service, *Tax Exempt Status for Your Organization* (Washington, DC: Department of the Treasury, 2016), https://www.irs.gov/pub/irs-pdf/p557.pdf.

8.   In 2014 alone, 1,966 pastors participated in Pulpit Freedom Sunday. Thirty-three pastors participated in the first Pulpit Freedom Sunday in 2008.

9.   Wayne Laugesen, "Suit to Dismiss Pulpit Speech Dismissed," *National Catholic Register,* September 9, 2014, http://www.ncregister.com/daily-news/suit-to-restrict-pulpit-speech-dismissed.

10.   Romina Boccia, "How the United States' High Debt Will Weaken the Economy and Hurt Americans," *Backgrounder* 2786, Heritage Foundation, February 12, 2013, http://www.heritage.org/research/reports/2013/02/how-the-united-states-high-debt-will-weaken-the-economy-and-hurt-americans.

11.   Mark Hosenball, "U.S. Intelligence Chief Warns of 'Home-Grown' Security Threat," Reuters, February 9, 2016, http://www.reuters.com/article/us-usa-security-idUSKCN0VI1AQ.

12.   Angie Pettie, "Federal Government Continues to Lose Billions to Waste, Fraud, and Abuse," *Washington Post,* March 10, 2013, https://www.washingtonpost.com/business/capitalbusiness/federal-government-continues-to-lose-billions-to-waste-fraud-and-abuse/2013/03/08/a3fb7736-82b5-11e2-b99e-6baf4ebe42df_story.html.

13.   David A. Graham, "Motor City Meltdown," *Atlantic*, March 4, 2016, http://www.theatlantic.com/politics/archive/2016/03/republican-debate-detroit/472245/.

14.   T. M. Luhrmann, "The Anxious Americans," *New York Times*, July 18, 2015, http://www.nytimes.com/2015/07/19/opinion/sunday/the-anxious-americans.html.

15.   "Jefferson's Letter to the Danbury Baptists," Library of Congress, https://www.loc.gov/loc/lcib/9806/danpre.html.

16.   Daniel Dreisbach, *Thomas Jefferson and the Myth of Separation* (New York: University Press, 2002), 29.

17.   Ibid.

18.   Ibid.

19.   Learn more about the Jefferson Gathering at www.jeffersongathering. com.

CHAPTER TWO: WHY SHOULD ANYONE LISTEN TO ME?

1.   "What Does the Bible Say about Abortion?," Christian Bible Reference Site, http://www.christianbiblereference.org/faq_abortion.htm.

CHAPTER THREE: WHAT IS NEEDED NOW

1.   Micajah McPherson, "We Have Fought the Good Fight and Kept Our Faith," North Carolina Civil War Trails, *http://digital.ncdcr.gov/cdm/ref/collection/p15012coll8/id/10756*.

2.   Alecia Mackenzie, *Christian Post*, January 14, 2014.

3.   "Can the Graham Anointing Be Passed?," *Christianity Today*, April 5, 1999, http://www.christianitytoday.com/ct/1999/april5/9t4050. html.

4. United States Holocaust Memorial Museum, "Martin Niemöller: Biography," Holocaust Encyclopedia, January 14, 2014, https://www.ushmm.org/wlc/en/article.php?ModuleId=10007391.
5. "Religion: German Martyrs," *Time*, December 23, 1940, http://content.time.com/time/magazine/article/0,9171,765103,00.html.

CHAPTER FOUR: THE PURPOSE OF GOVERNMENT

1. "Benjamin Franklin's Great Seal Design," GreatSeal.com, http://greatseal.com/committees/firstcomm/reverse.html.
2. National African American History Month 2009," WhiteHouse.gov, February 2, 2009, https://www.whitehouse.gov/the-press-office/national-african-american-history-month-2009.
3. "Constitution Day, Citizenship Day, and Constitution Week," White House.gov, September 17, 2009, https://www.whitehouse.gov/the-press-office/presidential-proclamation-constitution-day-citizenship-day-and-constitution-week.
4. "Remarks by the President at the Congressional Hispanic Caucus Institute's 33rd Annual Awards Gala," WhiteHouse.gov, September 5, 2010, https://www.whitehouse.gov/the-press-office/2010/09/15/remarks-president-congressional-hispanic-caucus-institutes-33rd-annual-a.
5. "Remarks by the President at a DCCC/DSCC Dinner," WhiteHouse.gov, September 22, 2010, https://www.whitehouse.gov/the-press-office/2010/09/23/remarks-president-a-dcccdscc-dinner.
6. Lizzie Deardon, "ISIS 'Fatwa' on Female Sex Slaves Tells Militants How and When They Can Rape Captured Girls and Women," *Independent* (UK), www.independent.co.uk, December 29, 2015, http://www.independent.co.uk/news/world/middle-east/isis-fatwa-on-female-sex-slaves-tells-militants-how-and-when-they-can-rape-captured-women-and-girls-a6789036.html.

7. Malia Zimmerman, "74 Children Executed by ISIS for 'Crimes' That Include Refusal to Fast, Report Says," FoxNews.com, July 2, 2015, http://www.foxnews.com/world/2015/07/02/isis-executioners-spare-no-one-killing-74-children-for-crimes-including-not.html.

8. Dennis Prager, "If You Believe People Are Basically Good," December 21, 2002, http://www.dennisprager.com/if-you-believe-that-people-are-basically-good/.

9. Ibid.

10. Ibid.

11. Cass R. Sunstein, "Obama, FDR, and the Second Bill of Rights," Bloomberg View, January 28, 2013, http://www.bloombergview.com/articles/2013-01-28/obama-fdr-and-the-second-bill-of-rights.

CHAPTER FIVE: FIRST AMENDMENT AND RELIGIOUS LIBERTY

1. CNN Wire Staff, "Polygamist Leader Warren Jeffs Sentenced to Life in Prison," CNN.com, August 10, 2011, http://www.cnn.com/2011/CRIME/08/09/texas.polygamist.jeffs/.

2. National Archives, "The Declaration of Independence," http://www.archives.gov/exhibits/charters/declaration_transcript.html.

3. Daniel Blackman, "'British Values' Prevent More than Terrorism," MercatorNet, March 16, 2016, http://www.mercatornet.com/articles/view/the-uk-government-is-preventing-more-than-terrorism/17767.

4. Jason L. Riley, "Christian Belief Cost Kelvin Cochran His Job," *Wall Street Journal*, November 10, 2015, http://www.wsj.com/articles/christian-belief-cost-kelvin-cochran-his-job-1447200885

5. Conor Friedersdorf, "Refusing to Photograph a Gay Wedding Isn't Hateful," *Atlantic*, March 5, 2014, http://www.theatlantic.com/politics/archive/2014/03/refusing-to-photograph-a-gay-wedding-isnt-hateful/284224/.

CHAPTER SIX: SCHOOLS, UNIVERSITIES, AND THE CHRISTIAN FAITH

1. Benjamin Franklin, cited in C. N. Douglas, *Forty Thousand Quotations: Prose and Poetical* (London: George G. Harrap, 1917).

2. Barna Group, "Public Schools: Christians Are Part of the Solution," Research Release, Barna, August 26, 2014, https://www.barna.org/barna-update/culture/681-public-schools-christians-are-part-of-the-solution#.VCJCZ1ayjwI.

3. Werner Lumm, "A Christian Philosophy of Education and John Dewey," BJU Press, October 21, 2015, https://www.bjupress.com/resources/articles/t2t/a-christian-prespective-on-john-dewey.php.

4. Abington School District v. Schempp, 374 U.S. 203, 226–227 (1963).

5. Stone v. Graham, 449 U.S. 39 (1980)

6. Wallace v. Jaffree, 472 U.S., 38, 61 (1985).

7. Lee v. Weisman, 505 U.S. 577, 599 (1992).

8. Santa Fe Independent School Dist. v. Doe, 530 U.S. 290, 2000.

9. Jason Kandel and Tony Shin, "Teacher Tells Student Not to Talk about Bible in School: Lawyer," NBC4 Southern California, January 14, 2014, http://www.nbclosangeles.com/news/local/Student-Not-Allowed-Talk-About-Bible-School-Lawyer-240195351.html.

10. Jordan Rudner, "Cheerleader Case Can Proceed, State Supreme Court Rules," *Texas Tribune*, January 29, 2016, http://www.texastribune.org/2016/01/29/cheerleaders-bible-verse-can-proceed-state-supreme/.

11. Cheryl Wetzstein, "Praying Football Coach Files EEOC Complaint," *Washington Times*, December 15, 2015, http://www.washingtontimes.com/news/2015/dec/15/joe-kennedy-wash-football-coach-files-eeoc-complaint.

12. "ADF Lawsuit Results in Protection for Student Religious Expression at L.A. School District," news release, Alliance Defending Freedom, March 21, 2011, http://www.adfmedia.org/News/PRDetail/4611.

13. Todd Starnes, "School Bans Christian Club, Again," FoxNews.com, October 6, 2014, http://www.foxnews.com/opinion/2014/10/06/school-bans-christian-club-again.html.

14. David Barton, *America: To Pray or Not to Pray?* (Aledo, TX: Wall-Builder Press, 1988).

15. Dan Graves, "A College Named for John Harvard," Christianity.com, October 6, 2014, http://www.christianity.com/church/church-history/timeline/1601-1700/a-college-named-for-john-harvard-11630093.html.

16. Harvard GSAS Christian Community, "Shield and 'Veritas' History," October 6, 2014, http://www.hcs.harvard.edu/~gsascg/shield-and-veritas-history/.

17. Samuel E. Morrison, *The Founding of Harvard College* (Cambridge, MA: Harvard University Press, 2015), 333.

18. Dan Oren, "Stamp of Approval," *Yale Alumni Magazine*, March 2001, http://archives.yalealumnimagazine.com/issues/01_03/seal.html.

19. Collin Hansen, "The Holy and the Ivy," *Christianity Today*, September 1, 2005, http://www.christianitytoday.com/ct/2005/september/26/64.html.

20. Ellis Washington, "Harvard, the Ivy League, and the Forgotten Puritans," WorldNetDaily.com, June 30, 2007, http://www.wnd.com/2007/06/423438/.

21. J. C. Derrick, "Two Schools Leave CCCU—for Opposite Reasons," *World*, December 11, 2015, http://www.worldmag.com/2015/12/two_schools_leave_cccu_for_opposite_reasons.

22. The Council for Christian Colleges and Universities (CCCU) is a higher education association of 180 Christian institutions around the world, https:///www.cccu.org/members_and_affiliates.

23. Bob Smietana, "Oklahoma Wesleyan and Union U. Quit CCCU over Same-Sex Marriage Moves," *Christianity Today*, August 31, 2015,

http://www.christianitytoday.com/ct/2015/august-web-only/union-university-quits-cccu-same-sex-marriage.html.

24. Jeremy Weber, "Peace Church Out: Mennonite Schools Leave CCCU to Avoid Same-Sex Marriage Split," *Christianity Today*, September 21, 2015, http://www.christianitytoday.com/gleanings/2015/september/cccu-emu-goshen-college-okwu-union-membership-status.html; and Derrick, "Two Schools Leave CCCU."

25. Conversation between Jim Garlow and Dr. Everett Piper.

CHAPTER SEVEN: POLITICAL CORRECTNESS

1. Thomas Sowell, "Random Thoughts," *Jewish World Review*, September 21, 2005, http://www.jewishworldreview.com/cols/sowell092105.asp.

2. Charlton Heston, speech at the Harvard Law School, 1999, as quoted in Richard Corliss, "Appreciation: Charlton Heston" *Time*, April 6, 2008, http://content.time.com/time/arts/article/0,8599,1728272,00.html.

3. Georg Lukacs, *Theory of the Novel* (Berlin: P. Cassirer, 1920), 11.

4. Herbert Marcuse, "Eros and Civilization," 1955, available at Marxists.org, https://www.marxists.org/reference/archive/marcuse/works/eros-civilisation/epilogue.htm.

5. Eric Fromm, *The Art of Loving* (New York: Harper & Roe, 1956).

6. Robert Paul Wolff, Barrington Moore Jr., and Herbert Marcuse, *A Critique of Pure Tolerance* (Boston: Beacon Press, 1969), 95–137.

7. Alliance Defending Freedom (ADF) is presently handling many of these cases. See *State of Washington v. Arlene's Flowers*, http://www.adfmedia.org/News/PRDetail/8608; *Masterpiece Cakeshop v. Craig*, http://www.adfmedia.org/News/PRDetail/8700; and *Elane Photography v. Willock*, http://www.adfmedia.org/news/prdetail/5537.

8.   See the "Cenzon-DeCarlo v. Mt. Sinai Hospital Resource Page," Alliance Defending Freedom, updated February 12, 2013, http://www.adfmedia.org/news/prdetail/2895.

9.   Todd Starnes, "Baker Forced to Make Gay Wedding Cakes, Undergoing Sensitivity Training, After Losing Lawsuit," FoxNews.com, June 3, 2014, http://www.foxnews.com/opinion/2014/06/03/baker-forced-to-make-gay-wedding-cakes-undergo-sensitivity-training-after.html.

CHAPTER EIGHT: MARRIAGE

1.   "The Supreme Court Has Ruled. What's Next?," Focus on the Family, no date, http://www.focusonthefamily.com/socialissues/promos/supreme-court-marriage-decision.

2.   Ryan Anderson, "In-Depth: 4 Harms the Court's Marriage Ruling Will Cause," Daily Signal, June 30, 2015, http://dailysignal.com/2015/06/30/in-depth-4-harms-the-courts-marriage-ruling-will-cause/.

3.   Ballotpedia, "California Proposition 22, Limit on Marriages (2000)," June 30, 2015, https://ballotpedia.org/California_Proposition_22,_Limit_on_Marriages_(2000).

4.   Jennifer Marshall, Daniel P. Moloney, and Matthew Spalding, "California Court's Judicial Activism Threatens the Institution of Marriage," Heritage Foundation, May 20, 2008, http://www.heritage.org/research/reports/2008/05/california-courts-judicial-activism-threatens-the-institution-of-marriage.

5.   Gregory B. Lewis and Charles W. Gossett, "Why Did Californians Pass Proposition 8? Stability and Change in Public Support for Same-Sex Marriage," *California Journal of Politics & Policy* 3, no. 1 (2011): http://scholarworks.gsu.edu/cgi/viewcontent.cgi?article=1002&context=pmap_facpubs.

6.   Jesse McKinley and Kirk Johnson, "Mormons Tipped Scale in Ban on Gay Marriage," *New York Times*, November 14, 2008, http://www.nytimes.com/2008/11/15/us/politics/15marriage.html?_r=0.

7.   Ibid.

8.   John Schwartz, "California High Court Upholds Gay Marriage Ban," *New York Times*, May 26, 2009, http://www.nytimes.com/2009/05/27/us/27marriage.html.

9.   Jesse McKinley and John Schwartz, "Court Rejects Same-Sex Marriage Ban in California," *New York Times*, August 4, 2010, http://www.nytimes.com/2010/08/05/us/05prop.html?pagewanted=all.

10.   Maura Dolan, "Prop 8: Gay Marriages Can Resume in California, Court Rules," *Los Angeles Times*, June 28, 2013, http://articles.latimes.com/2013/jun/28/local/la-me-ln-prop-8-gay-marriage-20130628.

11.   Howard Mintz, "California Supreme Court Jumps Back into Gay-Marriage Fray," *San Jose Mercury-News*, February 16, 2011, http://www.mercurynews.com/breaking-news/ci_17404629.

12.   Schwartz, "Between the Lines of the Proposition 8 Opinion," *Los Angeles Times*, June 26, 2013, http://www.nytimes.com/interactive/2013/06/26/us/annotated-supreme-court-decision-on-proposition-8.html.

13.   John Eastman, "The Constitutionality of Traditional Marriage," Heritage Foundation, January 25, 2013, http://www.heritage.org/research/reports/2013/01/the-constitutionality-of-traditional-marriage.

CHAPTER NINE: SCHOOL CHOICE AND PARENTAL AUTHORITY

1.   "From George Washington to George Chapman, 15 December 1784," Founders.Archives.Gov.

2.   "It shall be an infraction for any person to perform or offer to perform body piercing upon a person under the age of 18 years, unless the body piercing is performed in the presence of, or as directed by a notarized

writing by, the person's parent or guardian." State Legislature of California, California Penal Code 652-652, http://www.co.fresno.ca.us/ uploadedFiles/Departments/Public_Health/Divisions/CH/content/CD/ content/Outreach_Surveilance_Investigation/10020_PENAL percent 20CODE652653.pdf.

3.   "The health care provider is not permitted to inform a parent or legal guardian [of an abortion] without minor's consent." See State Legislature of California, California Minor Consent Laws, http:// www.csus.edu/indiv/b/brocks/Courses/EDS percent20245/Handouts/ Week percent207/CA_Minor_Consent.pdf.

4.   Christopher Coble, "Abortion Laws by State," FindLaw, January 27, 2016, http://blogs.findlaw.com/law_and_life/2016/01/abortion-laws-by-state.html.

5.   Ibid.

6.   Alex Newman, "Feds Seek Home Visits, Calling Parents 'Equal Partners,'" *New American*, February 11, 2016, http://www.thenewamerican.com/ culture/family/item/22530-feds-seek-home-visits-calling-parents-equal-partners.

7.   "Humanist Manifesto I," AmericanHumanist.org., http://american humanist.org/humanism/humanist_manifesto_i.

8.   Henry M. Morris, "The Evolving Humanist Manifestos," *Acts & Facts*. 32, no. 10 (2003).

9.   Dewey said, "Abandon the notion of subject-matter as something fixed and ready-made in itself, outside the child's experience [...]; and we realize that the child and the curriculum are simply two limits which define a single process." John Dewey, *The Child and the Curriculum* (Chicago: University of Chicago Press, 1902), 16.

10.   Sam Weaver, "John Dewey: The Father of Progressive Education," Renew America, March 8, 2004, http://www.renewamerica.com/ columns/weaver/040308.

11.   Jimmy Carter, "Department of Education Organization Act Statement on Signing S. 210 Into Law," October 17, 1979, available online at

American Presidency Project, http://www.presidency.ucsb.edu/ws/
?pid=31543.

12. "How Does the Department of Education Serve America's Students?"
U.S. Department of Education, http://www2.ed.gov/about/overview/
focus/what_pg3.html#howdoes.

13. Public Law 96-88—OCT. 17, 1979," available online at https://history.
nih.gov/research/downloads/PL96-88.pdf.

14. *A Growing Movement: America's Largest Charter School Communities*
(Washington, DC: National Alliance for Public Charter Schools,
December 2014), http://www.publiccharters.org/wp-content/uploads
/2014/12/2014_Enrollment_Share_FINAL.pdf.

15. National Alliance for Public Charter Schools, "Charter School
Enrollment up 13 percent This Year," news release, February 12, 2014,
http://www.publiccharters.org/press/charter-school-enrollment-13-
percent-year/.

16. "Growth and Enrollment," California Charter Schools Association,
http://www.ccsa.org/understanding/numbers/.

17. Ibid.

CHAPTER TEN: ABORTION

1. Presidential Debate in Baltimore, September 21, 1980, available online
at the American President Project, http://www.presidency.ucsb.edu/
ws/index.php?pid=29407.

2. Totals as of March 25, 2016 from http://www.numberofabortions.
com/.

3. "Baby Developmental Facts," ProLife Across America, no date, https://
prolifeacrossamerica.org/baby-developmental-facts/.

4. Steven Ertelt, "Woman Behind Roe v. Wade: 'I'm Dedicating My Life
to Overturning It,'" LifeNews.com, January 22, 2013, http://www.

lifenews.com/2013/01/22/woman-behind-roe-v-wade-im-dedicating-my-life-to-overturning-it/.

5. Jeani Change, "Morbidity and Mortality Weekly Report," Center for Disease Control and Prevention, February 21, 2003, http://www.cdc.gov/mmwr/pdf/ss/ss5202.pdf.

6. A. Torres and J. Forest, "Why Do Women Have Abortions?" *Family Planning Perspectives* 20, no. 4 (July–August, 1988): 169–76.

7. A. Bankole et al., "Reasons Why Women Have Induced Abortions: Evidence from 27 Countries," *Family Planning Perspectives* 24, no. 3 (August 1998): 117–25, 152.

8. Gregory S. Baylor, "Feds Force Insurance Coverage of Contraceptives and Abortifacients," Alliance Defending Freedom, January 20, 2012, https://adflegal.org/detailspages/blog-details/allianceedge/2012/01/20/feds-force-insurance-coverage-of-contraceptives-and-abortifacients.

9. "Faith and Justice Details Fault Lines," *Faith and Justice* 3 no. 2, http://www.adflegal.org/detailspages/faith-and-justice-details/fault-lines.

10. Lydia Saad, "Public Opinion about Abortion: An In-Depth Review," Gallup.com, January 22, 2002, http://www.gallup.com/poll/9904/public-opinion-about-abortion-indepth-review.aspx.

11. Ibid.

12. Saad, "Generational Differences on Abortion Narrow," Gallup.com, March 12, 2010, http://www.gallup.com/poll/126581/Generational-Differences-Abortion-Narrow.aspx.

13. "Abortion Statistics," National Right to Life, no date, http://www.nrlc.org/communications/abortionnumbers/.

14. Ibid.

CHAPTER ELEVEN: SEXUAL ORIENTATION AND GENDER IDENTITY

1. Chanel Adams, "Miley Cyrus GenderQueer? Singer Reveals Her Gender Identity and Sexuality," *Inquisitr*, May 6, 2015, http://www. inquisitr.com/2070730/miley-cyrus-genderqueer-singer-reveals-her-gender-identity-and-sexuality/#i5oGYSb93fMfUpJL.99.

2. Emily James, "I've Gone Back to Being a Child," Daily Mail, December 11, 2015, http://www.dailymail.co.uk/femail/article-3356084/I-ve-gone-child-Husband-father-seven-52-leaves-wife-kids-live-transgender-SIX-YEAR-OLD-girl-named-Stefonknee.html.

3. Peter Weber, "Confused by All the New Facebook Genders? Here's What They Mean," Dialy Mail, February 21, 2014, http://www.slate.com/blogs/lexicon_valley/2014/02/21/gender_facebook_now_has_56_categories_to_choose_from_including_cisgender.html.

4. Sean Dooley, Margaret Dawson, Lana Zak, Christina Ng, Lauren Effron, and Meghan KeNeally, "Bruce Jenner: 'I'm A Woman,'"ABC. com, August 24, 2015, http://abcnews.go.com/Entertainment/bruce-jenner-im-woman/story?id=30570350.

5. Buzz Bissinger, "Caitlyn Jenner: The Full Story," *Vanity Fair*, June 25, 2015, http://www.vanityfair.com/hollywood/2015/06/caitlyn-jenner-bruce-cover-annie-leibovitz.

6. Christopher Rosen, "Caitlyn Jenner Will Receive Arthur Ashe Award for Courage at This Year's ESPYs," June 1, 2015, *Entertainment Weekly*, http://www.ew.com/article/2015/06/01/caitlyn-jenner-espys.

7. Danica Lo, "Caitlyn Jenner *Glamour* Women of the Year 2015 Award Acceptance Speech," *Glamour*, November 10, 2015, http://www.glamour.com/inspired/blogs/the-conversation/2015/11/caitlyn jenner-speech.

8. Allison Corneau, "Caitlyn Jenner: Giving ESPYS Arthur Ashe Courage Award Speech 'Wasn't Easy,'" *US Weekly*, July 16, 2015, http://www.usmagazine.com/celebrity-news/news/caitlyn-jenner-giving-espys-courage-award-speech-wasnt-easy-2015167.

9.   The first appearance of the word "homosexual" was in the *New York Medical Journal*, April 22, 1911.

10.   *Merriam-Webster*, s.v. "Gender," http://www.merriam-webster.com/dictionary/gender.

11.   *Merriam-Webster*, s.v. "Sex," http://www.merriam-webster.com/dictionary/sex.

12.   Ibid.

13.   Debby Herbenick and Aleta Baldwin, "What Each of Facebook's 51 New Gender Options Means," Daily Beast, February 15, 2014, http://www.thedailybeast.com/articles/2014/02/15/the-complete-glossary-of-facebook-s-51-gender-options.html.

14.   Ibid.

15.   Ibid.

16.   Shira Benozilio, "Miley Cyrus: My Gender Identity Is 'Fluid'—'I Don't Relate to Being Boy or Girl'," *Hollywood Life*, June 9, 2015, http://hollywoodlife.com/2015/06/09/miley-cyrus-gender-identity-fluid-boy-girl-paper-magazine-interview/.

17.   Jennifer Roback "Fifty Shades of Gay," Crisis, January 4, 2016, http://www.crisismagazine.com/2016/50-shades-of-gay.

18.   Ibid.

19.   Pickup v. Brown, No. 12-17681, U.S. Court of Appeals for the 9th Circuit, August 29, 2013.

20.   "Identical Twin Studies Prove Homosexuality Is Not Genetic," OrthodoxyNet.com, June 24, 2013, http://www.orthodoxytoday.org/blog/2013/06/identical-twin-studies-prove-homosexuality-is-not-genetic/.

21.   Lisa Penn, "Cheating Statistics: Do Men Cheat More Than Women?" *FoxNewsMagazine.com*, June 7, 2012 http://magazine.foxnews.com/love/cheating-statistics-do-men-cheat-more-women.

22.   "Porn Use and Addiction," ProvenMen.org, no date, http://www.provenmen.org/2014pornsurvey/pornography-use-and-addiction/.

23.   Maxwell Strachan, "Caitlyn Jenner Takes ESPYs by Storm: 'Trans People Deserve Something Vital. They Deserve Your Respect,'" Huffington Post, July 16, 2015, http://www.huffingtonpost.com/entry/caitlyn-jenner-espys-arthur-ashe-award_us_55a568a0e4b0896514cf9116.

24.   "NYC Commission on Human Rights Announces Strong Protections for City's Transgender and Gender Non-Conforming Communities in Housing, Employment and Public Spaces," NYC.gov, December 21, 2015, http://www1.nyc.gov/office-of-the-mayor/news/961-15/nyc-commission-human-rights-strong-protections-city-s-transgender-gender.

25.   Ibid.

26.   Chris Potts, "Previous Arrangements" *Faith & Justice* 7, no. 1, http://www.adflegal.org/detailspages/faith-and-justice-details/previous-arrangements.

27.   Emily Conley, "Ordinary People, Extraordinary Faith," Alliance Defending Freedom, December 8, 2015, https://www.adflegal.org/detailspages/blog-details/allianceedge/2015/12/08/ordinary-people-extraordinary-faith-blaine-adamson. See also "Lexington-Fayette Urban County Human Rights Commission v. Hands On Originals," February 9, 2016, http://www.adfmedia.org/News/PRDetail/9254.

28.   "Elane Photography v. Willock," Alliance Defending Media, April 7, 2014, http://www.adfmedia.org/news/prdetail/5537.

29.   "ADF Protecting Religious Liberty Internationally, Assisting Defense of Pastor in Sweden," November 9, 2005, http://www.adfmedia.org/News/PRDetail/1555?search=1".

30.   Matt Slick, "Genesis 18:20, 19:1–12, 24 and Sodom and Gomorrah," Christian Apologetics and Research Ministry, https://carm.org/sodom-gomorrah.

CHAPTER TWELVE: HEALTHCARE

1. Mark Twain, "Official Psychic," *New York Sunday Mercury*, April 21, 1867, http://www.twainquotes.com/mercury/OfficialPhysic.html.

2. "ADF to California Agency: You Cannot Force Employers to Cover Abortions," news release, Alliance Defending Freedom, August 22, 2014, http://www.adfmedia.org/News/PRDetail/9279.

3. "If You Don't Have Health Insurance: How Much You'll Pay," Healthcare. gov, https://www.healthcare.gov/fees/fee-for-not-being-covered/.

4. Laura Bassett, "Nuns Lose Case against Birth Control Mandate," Huffington Post, July 14, 2015, http://www.huffingtonpost.com/2015/07/14/little-sisters-of-the-poor_n_7796404.html.

5. Matt Bowman, "Conestoga and Hobby Lobby: The Aftermath Begins," *The Corner* (blog), *National Review*, July 1, 2014, http://www.nationalreview.com/corner/381668/conestoga-and-hobby-lobby-aftermath-begins-matt-bowman?target=topic&tid=2853.

6. "The HHS Mandate Isn't Fixed," Galen Institute, February 1, 2013, http://galen.org/topics/the-hhs-mandate-isn't-fixed/.

7. See www.numberofabortions.com. Number as of March 28, 2016.

8. Scott W. Atlas, "IPAB: President Obama's NICE Way to Ration Care for Seniors," *Forbes*, October 21, 2012, http://forbes.com/sites/scottatlas/2012/10/21/ipab-president-obamas-nice-way-to-ration-care-to-seniors/#1bda101a74f3.

9. Tom W. Howell Jr., "House Votes to Repeal Obamacare 'Death Panel,'" *Washington Times*, June 23, 2015, http://www.washingtontimes.com/news/2015/jun/23/death-panel-repealed-house-obamacare-vote/.

10. Julie Grace Brufke, "49 Out of 50 States Will See Individual Health Care Premiums Go Up in 2016," Daily Caller, January 11, 2016 http://dailycaller.com/2016/01/11/49-out-of-50-states-will-see-individual-health-care-premiums-go-up-in-2016/.

11. Tony Meggs, "Faith and Health Care Peacefully Coexist for Thousands of Americans," *Christian Post*, December 3, 2014, http://www. christianpost.com/news/faith-and-healthcare-peacefully-coexist-for-thousands-of-americans-130630/#cmYwwvwC151JLrJ9.99.

12. Lenny Bernstein, "U.S. Faces 90,000 Doctor Shortage by 2025, Medical School Association Warns," *Washington Post*, March 3, 2015, https://www.washingtonpost.com/news/to-your-health/wp/2015/03/03/u-s-faces-90000-doctor-shortage-by-2025-medical-school-association-warns/.

CHAPTER THIRTEEN: CAPITALISM AND SOCIALISM

1. Thomas Sowell, "The First Lesson of Economics Is Scarcity," *Imaginative Conservative*, October 26, 2012, http://www.theimaginative-conservative.org/2012/10/the-first-lesson-of-economics-is-html.

2. Adam Smith, *An Inquiry into the Nature and Causes of the Wealth of Nations*, vol. II (London: W. Strahan and T. Cadell, 1778), 35.

3. The Declaration of Independence, National Archives, http://www. archives.gov/exhibits/charters/declaration_transcript.html.

4. John Locke, *Two Treatises on Government* (London: R. Butler, 1821), 259.

5. Michael Tanner, "Capitalism's Triumph," *National Review*, September 18, 2013, http://nationalreview.com/article/358771/capitalisms-triumph-michael-tanner.

6. John Wesley, "The Use of Money," Global Ministries of the United Methodist Church, September 18, 2013, http://umcmission.org/Find-Resources/John-Wesley-Sermons/Sermon-50-The-Use-of-Money.

7. Tim Haims, "Obama: Forget the Difference Between Capitalism and Communism: 'Just Decide What Works,'" RealClearPolitics, March 25, 2016, http://www.realclearpolitics.com/video/2016/03/25/obama_forget_the_difference_between_capitalism_and_communism_just_decide_what_works.html.

8. Ibid.

9. Karl Marx and Fredrich Engels, *On Religion* (Mineola, NY: Dover Publications, 2008), 42.

10. Marx and Engels, *The Communist Manifesto* (London: Penguin Books, 2011).

11. "Socialism Is the Philosophy of Failure," Churchill Project at Hillsdale College, http://winstonchurchill.hillsdale.edu/socialism-is-the-philosophy-of-failure-winston-churchill/.

12. Ibid.

13. As of March 28, 2016, the U.S. Debt Clock read $19,203,445,200.00, http://www.usdebtclock.org.

CHAPTER FOURTEEN: TAXES

1. Quoted by Cindy Perman in "Taxes Are Hilarious: From Ronald Reagan to Jay Leno," CNBC.com, April 13, 2011, http://www.cnbc.com/id/42571251.

2. Winston Churchill, "Why I Believe in Free Trade," *Tom Watson's Magazine* 2 (July 1905): 64, https://play.google.com/store/books/details?id=BE5TAAAAYAAJ&rdid=book-BE5TAAAAYAAJ&rdot=1.

3. Quoted by Jonah Goldberg in "The Surplus Is Your Money!," *National Review*, August 23, 2000, http://www.nationalreview.com/article/204713/surplus-your-money-jonah-goldberg.

4. The overall gist of this statement comes from Ronald Reagan's speech "A Time for Choosing," October 27, 1964, available online at the Reagan Library, https://reaganlibrary.archives.gov/archives/reference/timechoosing.html.

5. "Polycarp-Martyrdom," Polycarp.net, no date, http://www.polycarp.net/.

6. *Oxford Biblical Studies Online*, s.v., "Emperor Worship," www.oxfordbiblicalstudies.com/article/opr/t94/e602.

7.   Kelly Phillips Erb, "Our Current Tax v. The Flat Tax v. The Fair Tax: What's the Difference?" *Forbes*, August 7, 2015, http://www.forbes.com/sites/kellyphillipserb/2015/08/07/our-current-tax-v-the-flat-tax-v-the-fair-tax-whats-the-difference/#422e0b291fa6.

8.   "Transcript of Republican Presidential Debate: Cleveland, Ohio," *Time*, August 6, 2015, http://time.com/3988276/republican-debate-primetime-transcript-full-text/.

9.   "2015 Federal Tax Rates, Personal Exemptions, and Standard Deductions: IRS Tax Brackets and Deduction Amounts for Tax Year 2015," IRS.com, https://www.irs.com/articles/2015-federal-tax-rates-personal-exemptions-and-standard-deductions.

10. For an extensive discussion about the relationship between the poll tax and the tithe, see Edward McGlynn Gaffney Jr., "Religious Autonomy and the Exemption of Religious Organizations from Federal Taxation in the United States," 1999, https://www.uni-trier.de/fileadmin/fb5/inst/IEVR/Arbeitsmaterialien/Staatskirchenrecht/Europa/Conference_1999/gaffney.pdf.

11. McCulloch v. Maryland, 17 U.S. 316 (1819), https://www.oyez.org/cases/1789-1850/17us316.

12. "Demographic Statistics," Infoplease.com, http://www.infoplease.com/us/census/data/demographic.html.

CHAPTER FIFTEEN: DEBT

1.   George Washington, "Farewell Address, 1796," available online at http://avalon.law.yale.edu/18th_century/washing.asp.

2.   Romina Boccia, "Federal Spending by the Numbers, 2014: Government Spending Trends in Graphics, Tables, and Key Points (Including 51 Examples of Government Waste)," Heritage Foundation, December 8, 2014, http://www.heritage.org/research/reports/2014/12/federal-spending-by-the-numbers-2014.

3. Ian Schwartz, "Flashback: Obama Talks 'Unpatriotic' Debt in 2008," RealClearPolitics, March 13, 2013, http://www.realclearpolitics.com/video/2011/08/24/flashback_obama_adding_4_trillion_to_debt_is_unpatriotic.html.

4. Dave Boyer, "$20 Trillion Man: National Debt Nearly Doubles during Obama Presidency," *Washington Times*, November 1, 2015, http://www.washingtontimes.com/news/2015/nov/1/obama-presidency-to-end-with-20-trillion-national-/.

5. Excerpt from Adam Smith [George J. W. Goodman], *Paper Money*, available online at PBS.org, http://www.pbs.org/wgbh/commanding heights/shared/minitext/ess_germanhyperinflation.html.

6. Total from http://www.usdebtclock.org/ as of April 2, 2016.

7. Ibid.

8. Schwartz, "Flashback."

9. Elmer T. Peterson, "This Is the Hard Core of Freedom," *Daily Oklahoman*, December 9, 1951. While this statement has been attributed to Alexis d' Tocqueville, it has also been attributed to Alexander Fraser Tytler. The first known source of the quote is in the article cited above.

CHAPTER SIXTEEN: WELFARE AND WORKFARE

1. Dr. Thomas Sowell, "Liberalism vs. Blacks," CreatorsSyndicate.com, January 15, 2013, https://www.creators.com/read/thomas-sowell/01/13/liberalism-versus-blacks.

2. Kristina Ribali, "5 Crazy Examples of Welfare Fraud and the 3-Step Solution for States to Stop the Scam," Foundation for Government Accountability, April 2, 2015, http://thefga.org/press/for-immediate-release-5-crazy-examples-of-welfare-fraud-and-the-3-step-solution-for-states-to-stop-the-scam/.

3.   Robert Rector and Rachel Sheffield, "The War on Poverty After 50 Years," Heritage Foundation, September 15, 2014, http://www. heritage.org/research/reports/2014/09/the-war-on-poverty-after-50-years.

4.   Star Parker, "Fighting Poverty with Real American Values," Center for Urban Renewal and Education, January 12, 2016, http://www. urbancure.org/mbarticle.asp?id=737&t=Fighting-poverty-with-real-American-values.

5.   Ibid.

6.   Ibid.

7.   John F. Harris and John E. Yang, "Clinton to Sign Bill Overhauling Welfare," *Washington Post*, August 1, 1996, http://www.washingtonpost. com/wp-srv//welfare/stories/wf080196.htm.

8.   Robert A. Moffitt, "The Temporary Assistance for Needy Families Act," in *Means-Tested Transfer Programs in the United States* (University of Chicago Press, 2003), http://www.nber.org/books/ moff03-1.

9.   Jennifer Rubin, "Obama to Clinton Welfare Reform: Drop Dead," *Washington Post*, July 15, 2013, https://www.washingtonpost.com/blogs/ right-turn/post/obama-to-clinton-welfare-reform-drop-dead/2012/07/14/ gJQAM49XkW_blog.html.

10.   Joe Hoft, "After Obamacare, Six Things You Need to Know," Gateway Pundit, June 1, 2015, http://www.thegatewaypundit.com/2015/06/ after-six-years-of-obamanomics-five-things-you-need-to-know/.

11.   "Only Half of Protestant Pastors Have a Biblical Worldview," Barna. org, January 12, 2004, https://www.barna.org/component/content/ article/5-barna-update/45-barna-update-sp-657/133-only-half-of-protestant-pastors-have-a-biblical-worldview#.VwCVzE3mrIU.

12.   Parker, "Fighting Poverty with Real American Values."

CHAPTER SEVENTEEN: MINIMUM WAGE

1. Harvey Mackay, "The Single Best Way to Build Customer Loyalty," Inc.com, December 22, 2011, http://www.inc.com/harvey-mackay/best-way-to-build-customer-loyalty.html.

2. "Biographies: Henry Ford," History.co.uk, http://www.history.co.uk/biographies/henry-ford.

3. Taken from *Nelson's Illustrated Bible Dictionary* (Nashville: Thomas Nelson Publishers, 1986).

4. "John Wesley: The Methodist," Wesley Center Online, http://wesley.nnu.edu/john-wesley/john-wesley-the-methodist/chapter-x-lay-helpers/; James L. Garlow, "John Wesley's Understanding of the Laity as Demonstrated by His Use of the Lay Preachers," Drew University, Madison, New Jersey, 1979.

5. I am indebted to Dennis Peacocke for many conversations about the above principles. He has been my teacher. I have been his student, both in person and over the phone, sometimes in lengthy conversations as he taught biblical principles. In the 1970s, Dennis was a left-wing socialist, a student at the University of California, Berkeley, and an economics major. Christ got a hold of his life, and he was transformed. He is an accomplished thinker, lecturer, writer, and mentor. He now travels all over the world demonstrating the biblical principles of economics. For more information about Dennis Peacocke, go to http://www.gostrategic.org/about-dennis/ and become familiar with the "Statesman Project," a creative training model designed to equip the church to understand scriptural economic principles.

6. "Hobby Lobby Media Information and Fact Sheet," BecketFund.org, http://www.becketfund.org/hobbylobbyfactsheet/.

7. Emily Hulsey, "When Hobby Lobby's Critics Find Out How Much It Pays Employees, They Might Want to Get a Job There," Independent Journal, July 2014, http://www.ijreview.com/2014/07/152495-hobby-lobbys-haters-find-much-pays-employees-may-just-want-get-job/.

CHAPTER EIGHTEEN: SOCIAL SECURITY

1. Tia Walker and Peggy Speers, *The Inspired Caregiver: Finding Joy While Caring for Those You Love* (North Charleston, SC: CreateSpace Independent Publishing Platform, 2013). Also see http://theinspired-caregiver.com/blog/?page_id=1651.

2. "Policy Basics: Where Do Our Federal Tax Dollars Go?," Center on Budget and Policy Priorities, March 4, 2016, http://www.cbpp.org/research/federal-budget/policy-basics-where-do-our-federal-tax-dollars-go.

3. "Social Security Fact Sheet," Committee for a Responsible Federal Budget, March 15, 2016, http://crfb.org/category/issue-area/social-security.

4. Social Security and Medicare Boards of Trustees, "A Summary of 2015 Annual Reports," Social Security Administration, https://www.ssa.gov/oact/trsum.

5. Veronique de Rugy, "How Many Workers Support One Social Security Retiree?," George Mason University Mercatus Center, May 22, 2012, http://mercatus.org/publication/how-many-workers-support-one-social-security-retiree.

6. Gary Foreman, "16 Facts You Need to Know about Social Security—No Matter How Old You Are," *Money* (blog), *U.S. News & World Report*, October 25, 2012, http://money.usnews.com/money/blogs/my-money/2012/10/25/16-facts-you-need-to-know-about-social-securityno-matter-how-old-you-are.

7. Social Security Administration, "Life Expectancy for Social Security," https://www.ssa.gov/history/lifeexpect.html.

8. Number as of March 28, 2016, from www.numberofabortions.com.

CHAPTER NINETEEN: THE JUDICIARY

1. Jeffrey Rosen, "The Dangerous Doctrine of a Constitutional 'Right to Dignity,'" *Atlantic*, April 29, 2015, http://www.theatlantic.com/politics/archive/2015/04/the-dangerous-doctrine-of-dignity/391796/.

2. Sean Davis, "Supreme Court Declares Same-Sex Marriage a Constitutional Right," Federalist, June 26, 2015, http://the federalist.com/2015/06/26/supreme-court-declares-same-sex-marriage-a-constitutional-right/.

3. "Roe v. Wade," Heritage Foundation Rule of Law Initiative, no date, http://www.heritage.org/initiatives/rule-of-law/judicial-activism/cases/roe-v-wade.

4. James A. Cox, "Bilboes, Brands, and Banks," *Colonial Williamsburg Journal*, Spring 2003: http://www.history.org/foundation/journal/spring03/branks.cfm.

5. Charles Evans Hughes, speech before the Chamber of Commerce, Elmira, New York, May 3, 1907, in *Addresses and Papers of Charles Evans Hughes, Governor of New York, 1906–1908* (New York: G. P. Putnam's Sons, 1908), 139.

6. "Thomas Jefferson: Domestic Affairs," Miller Center at University of Virginia, June 26, 2015, http://millercenter.org/president/biography/jefferson-domestic-affairs.

7. Selwyn Duke, "Ted Cruz: President Can Ignore Unconstitutional Supreme Court Decisions," *New American*, December 10, 2015, http://www.thenewamerican.com/usnews/politics/item/22111-ted-cruz-president-can-ignore-unconstitutional-supreme-court-decisions.

8. Christopher Ingraham, "Why It's Time to Get Serious about Supreme Court Term Limits," *Washington Post*, February 13, 2016, https://www.washingtonpost.com/news/wonk/wp/2016/02/13/why-its-time-to-get-serious-about-supreme-court-term-limits/.

9.   Andrew S. Gold, "Appellate Jurisdiction Clause," Heritage Foundation, http://www.heritage.org/constitution/#!/articles/3/essays/117/appellate-jurisdiction-clause.

CHAPTER TWENTY: HATE CRIMES

1.   Thomas Sowell, "Random Thoughts," Jewish World Review, January 4, 1999, http://www.jewishworldreview.com/cols/sowell010499.asp.
2.   "Hate Crimes—Overview," Federal Bureau of Investigation, https://www.fbi.gov/about-us/investigate/civilrights/hate_crimes/overview.
3.   "ADF Protecting Religious Liberty Internationally, Assisting Defense of Pastor in Sweden," Alliance Defending Freedom, November 9, 2005, http://www.adfmedia.org/News/PRDetail/1555?search=1.
4.   Alliance Defending Freedom Chief Counsel Benjamin W. Bull assisted with Pastor Green's defense and was present at the Swedish Supreme Court when the prosecutor made this statement.

CHAPTER TWENTY-ONE: SOCIAL JUSTICE

1.   Gary DeMar, "Social Justice Is Wealth Distribution," July 14, 2012, http://godfatherpolitics.com/social-justice-is-wealth-distribution/.
2.   Robert Sirico, "'Social Justice' Is a Complex Concept," *Religion & Liberty* 21, no. 1: http://www.acton.org/pub/religion-liberty/volume-21-number-1/social-justice-complex-concept.
3.   Pope Leo XIII, "Rerum Novarum: Encyclical of Pope Leo XIII on Capital and Labor," May 15, 1891, http://w2.vatican.va/content/leo-xiii/en/encyclicals/documents/hf_l-xiii_enc_15051891_rerum-novarum.html.

4.   Joshua J. McElwee, "Pope Meets with Liberation Theology Pioneer," *National Catholic Reporter*, September 25, 2013, http://ncronline. org/news/theology/pope-meets-liberation-theology-pioneer.

5.   "The Declaration of Independence," National Archives, http://www. archives.gov/exhibits/charters/declaration_transcript.html.

6.   BusinessDictionary.com, s.v. "Social Justice," http://www.business dictionary.com/definition/social-justice.html.

7.   Willis L. Krumholz, "Five Reasons America Needs More Dads," Federalist, May 2, 2014, http://thefederalist.com/2014/05/22/five-reasons-america-needs-more-dads/.

8.   W. B. Wilcox, Robert I. Lerman, and Joseph Price, "Strong Families, Prosperous States: Do Healthy Families Affect the Wealth of States?," American Enterprise Institute, October 19, 2015, https://www.aei. org/publication/strong-families-prosperous-states/.

9.   Nick Chiles, "7 Ways the War on Poverty Destroyed Black Fatherhood," *Atlanta Black Star*, December 24, 2014, http://atlanta blackstar.com/2014/12/24/ways-war-poverty-destroyed-black-fatherhood/.

CHAPTER TWENTY-TWO: RACISM, JUDICIAL AND PRISON REFORM

1.   Martin Luther King, "I Have a Dream," August 28, 1963, available online at http://www.usconstitution.net/dream.html.

2.   Kweku Mandela quoted his father Nelson Mandela in "Remembering Nelson Mandela," Benedictine University, December 4, 2014, http:// www.cvdl.org/blog/remembering-nelson-mandela/.

3.   Noah Rothman "Poll: Race Relations Were Better under Bush," HotAir.com, August 26, 2014, http://hotair.com/archives/2014/08/26/ poll-race-relations-were-better-under-bush/.

4.   "Race Relations," Gallup.com, http://www.gallup.com/poll/1687/ race-relations.aspx.

5. Jesse Washington, "Blacks Struggle with 72 Percent Unwed Mothers Rate," NBC.com, November 7, 2010, http://www.nbcnews.com/id/39993685/ns/health-womens_health/t/blacks-struggle-percent-unwed-mothers-rate/.

6. Rachel Sheffield, "How Marriage, Strong Families Contribute to Economic Growth," Daily Signal, October 26, 2015, http://dailysignal.com/2015/10/26/how-marriage-strong-families-contribute-to-economic-growth/.

7. Clayton Youngman, "Potter's House Program Gives Texas Ex-offenders a Lift, Spiritually and Professionally," DallasNews.com, July 26, 2015, http://www.dallasnews.com/news/community-news/best-southwest/headlines/20150726-ex-offenders-in-texas-get-a-lift-spiritually-and-professionally.ece.

8. "Bishop TD Jakes Hosts as DA Hands Ex-offenders Diplomas instead of Sentences," news release, Potter's House, March 24, 2014, http://www.thepottershouse.org/PressRelease/BISHOP-TD-JAKES-HOSTS-AS-DA-HANDS-EX-OFFENDERS-DIPLOMAS-INSTEAD-OF-SENTENCES.aspx?cin=08c337af-3fa6-4fca-9d99-bea6f6de149d.

9. "Facts," Texas Offenders Reentry Initiative, http://medc-tori.org/.

10. All of the info regarding TORI came from a personal e-mail sent to Jim Garlow on March 31, 2016, from Tina Naidoo, executive director of TORI.

CHAPTER TWENTY-THREE: NATIONAL DEFENSE AND WAR

1. James Madison, "For the National Gazette, 31 January 1792," Founders.Archives.gov, http://founders.archives.gov/documents/Madison/01-14-02-0185.

2. George Washington, "From George Washington to the United States Senate and House of Representatives, 8 January 1790," Founders.Archives.gov, http://founders.archives.gov/documents/Washington/05-04-02-0361.

3.   Ronald Reagan, "Remarks on Signing the Intermediate Range Nuclear Forces Treaty," December 8, 1987, available online at https://reaganlibrary.archives.gov/archives/speeches/1987/120887c.htm.

CHAPTER TWENTY-FOUR: IMMIGRATION AND BORDER SECURITY

1.   "The President's News Conference," June 14, 1984, available online at http://www.presidency.ucsb.edu/ws/?pid=40049.
2.   Tony Blair, "Address to British Ambassadors," *Guardian* (UK), January 7, 2003 http://www.theguardian.com/politics/2003/jan/07/foreignpolicy.speeches
3.   Teresa Walsh, "5 Countries That Take the Most Immigrants," *U.S. News and World Report*, September 25, 2015, http://www.usnews.com/news/slideshows/5-countries-that-take-the-most-immigrants.
4.   Ruy Teixeira and Alan Abramowitz, "The Decline of the White Working Class and the Rise of a Mass Upper Middle Class," Brookings Institute, April 2008, http://www.brookings.edu/~/media/research/files/papers/2008/4/demographics-teixeira/04_demographics_teixeira.pdf.
5.   Catherine Collomp, "Unions, Civics, and National Identity," *Labor History* 29, no. 4 (Fall 1988) 450–74.
6.   "A Wesleyan View of Immigration," Wesleyan.org, https://www.wesleyan.org/237/a-wesleyan-view-of-immigration.
7.   Scott Greer, "According to Democrats, It's 'Un-American' to Enforce Immigration Laws," DailyCaller.com, March 22, 2016, http://dailycaller.com/2016/03/22/according-to-democrats-its-un-american-to-enforce-immigration-laws/.
8.   Sara Murray, "Many in U.S. Illegally Overstayed Their Visas," *Wall Street Journal*, April 7, 2013, http://www.wsj.com/articles/SB10001424127887323916304578404960101110032.

9. S.Res. 111: A Resolution Recognizing June 6, 2009, as the 70th Anniversary of the Tragic Date When the MS St. Louis, a Ship Carrying Jewish Refugees from Nazi Germany, Returned to Europe After Its Passengers Were Refused Admittance to the United States, https://www.congress.gov/bill/111th-congress/senate-resolution/111.

10. "Obama Quotes Nonexistent Bible Verse in Speech," *Week*, December 10, 2014, http://theweek.com/speedreads/440665/obama-quotes-nonexistent-bible-verse-immigration-speech.

11. President Barack Obama, "Remarks by the President in Address to the Nation on Immigration," WhiteHouse.gov, November 20, 2014, https://www.whitehouse.gov/the-press-office/2014/11/20/remarks-president-address-nation-immigration.

12. James Hoffmeier, *The Immigration Crisis: Immigrants, Aliens, and the Bible* (Wheaton, IL: Crossway Books, 2009), 52.

13. See Hoffmeier, *The Immigration Crisis*, 52, 89, 156 and elsewhere throughout the book.

CHAPTER TWENTY-FIVE: ISRAEL

1. John Adams, *The Works of John Adams, Ten Volumes* (Boston: Little and Brown, 1850–1856), IX, 609.

2. David Ben-Gurion, interview on CBS, October 5, 1956.

3. John Chrysostom, "Against the Jews. Homily 1," Tertullian.org, http://www.tertullian.org/fathers/chrysostom_adversus_judaeos_01_homily1.htm.

4. Gary Fuss, *The Joshua Accounts* (Xulon Press, 2012).

5. Martin Luther, "Martin Luther: 'The Jews & Their Lies,'" JewishVirtualLibrary.org, https://www.jewishvirtuallibrary.org/jsource/anti-semitism/Luther_on_Jews.html.

6. Harry Truman, "Draft of Recognition of Israel." TrumanLibrary.org, May 14, 1948.

7. Israel Ministry of Foreign Affairs, "5 Arab League Declaration on the Invasion of Palestine: 15 May 1948," http://www.mfa.gov.il/mfa/foreignpolicy/mfadocuments/yearbook1/pages/5 percent20arab percent20league percent20declaration percent20on percent20the percent20invasion percent20of percent20pales.aspx.

8. Lea Speyer, "Presbyterian Church USA Voted on Erasing 'Israel' from Prayers," Breaking Israel News, December 24, 2014, http://www.breakingisraelnews.com/26310/presbyterian-church-usa-voted-erasing-israel-prayers-biblical-zionism/#7oCQy9DGlSiuoOuT.97.

9. David Vejil, "Israel's Miracle Victory," *The Trumpet*, June 2007, https://www.thetrumpet.com/article/3636.24.95.0/world/israels-miracle-victory.

10. Harriet Sherwood, "Inside the Tunnels Hamas Built: Israel's Struggle against New Tactic in Gaza War," *Guardian* (UK), August 2, 2014, http://www.theguardian.com/world/2014/aug/02/tunnels-hamas-israel-struggle-gaza-war.

11. "The Peel Commission—1937," JewishVirtualLibrary.org, http://www.jewishvirtuallibrary.org/jsource/History/peel.html.

12. "Map of the U.N. Partition Plan—1947," JewishVirtualLibrary.org, http://www.jewishvirtuallibrary.org/jsource/History/partition_plan.html.

13. "The Khartoum Resolutions," JewishVirtualLibrary.org, http://www.jewishvirtuallibrary.org/jsource/Peace/three_noes.html.

14. David Shyovitz, "2000 Camp David Summit: Background and Overview," JewishVirtualLibrary.org, http://www.jewishvirtuallibrary.org/jsource/Peace/cd2000art.html.

15. Avi Isacharoff, "Revealed: Olmert's 2008 Peace Deal to the Palestinians," *Jerusalem Post*, May 24, 2013, http://www.jpost.com/Diplomacy-and-Politics/Details-of-Olmerts-peace-offer-to-Palestinians-exposed-314261; and Ethan Bronner, "Olmert Memoir Cites Near Deal for Mideast Peace," *New York Times*, January 27, 2011, http://www.nytimes.com/2011/01/28/world/middleeast/28mideast.html?_r=0.

16.   "The British Mandate," SimpleToRemember.com, http://www.
      simpletoremember.com/articles/a/the_british_mandate/.
17.   Ibid.
18.   Deroy Murdock, "Arabs Are Prominent in Israel's Government,"
      National Review, November 25, 2013, http://www.nationalreview.
      com/article/364746/arabs-are-prominent-israels-government-deroy-
      murdock.
19.   Ibid.
20.   Ibid.

CHAPTER TWENTY-SIX: THE ENVIRONMENT AND CLIMATE CHANGE

1.   "Czech President Says Ambitious Environmentalism Threatens Freedom
      and Democracy," Daily Mail, March 21, 2007, http://www.dailymail.
      co.uk/news/article-443806/Czech-president-says-ambitious-environ-
      mentalism-threatens-freedom-democracy.html#ixzz44pAWSldf.
2.   Thomas Sowell, "Global Warming Swindle," CreatorsSyndicate.com,
      March 14, 2007, https://www.creators.com/read/thomas-sowell/03/07/
      global-warming-swindle.
3.   Nigel Lawson, "Deep Thought: Climate of Superstition," *Spectator*,
      March 11, 2006, http://www.spectator.co.uk/2006/03/deep-thought-
      climate-of-superstition/.
4.   William Booth, "Al Gore, Sundance's Leading Man," *Washington
      Post*, January 26, 2006, http://www.washingtonpost.com/wp-dyn/
      content/article/2006/01/25/AR2006012502230.html.
5.   Jaclyn Schiff, "24 Days to Al Gore's 10 Years to Save the Planet and
      Point of No Return Planetary Emergency Deadline," FoxNews.com,
      January 2, 2016.
6.   Larry Bell, "The Greening of Gore's Bank Account," *Forbes*, May 21,
      2013, http://www.forbes.com/sites/larrybell/2013/05/21/the-greening-
      of-gores-bank-account/#215b51d5504f.

7.   David Whitehouse, *The Global Warming Standstill* (London: 2013, Global Warming Policy Foundation), http://www.thegwpf.org/content/uploads/2013/03/Whitehouse-GT_Standstill.pdf.

8.   "Antarctic Sea Ice Reaches New Maximum Extent," EarthObservatory. nasa.gov, October 1, 2013, http://earthobservatory.nasa.gov/IOTD/view.php?id=82160.

9.   Sean Davis, "Climate Change Is Real. Too Bad Accurate Climate Models Aren't," Federalist, May 6, 2014, http://thefederalist.com/2014/05/06/climate-change-is-real-too-bad-accurate-climate-models-arent/.

10. James Taylor, "Peer-Reviewed Survey Finds Majority of Scientists Skeptical of Global Warming Crisis," *Forbes*, February 13, 2013.

11. Global Warming Petition Project, http://www.petitionproject.org/.

12. U.S. Environment and Public Works Committee, "U.S. Senate Report: Over 400 Prominent Scientists Disputed Man-Made Global Warming Claims in 2007," December 20, 2007, http://www.epw.senate.gov/public/_cache/files/bba2ebce-6d03-48e4-b83c-44fe321a34fa/consensusbusterscompletedocument.pdf.

13. Larry Vardiman, "Does Carbon Dioxide Drive Global Warming?," Institute for Creation Research, *Acts & Facts* 37, no. 10 (2008).

14. Ibid.

CHAPTER TWENTY-SEVEN: ISLAM AND TERRORISM

1.   Cathleen Decker, "Rep. Loretta Sanchez: 'I've Never Attacked Muslims,'" *Los Angeles Times*, December 14, 2015, http://www.latimes.com/politics/la-pol-ca-loretta-sanchez-muslims-comment-201512 14-story.html.

2.   "About the List of Attacks," TheReligiousOfPeace.com, http://www.thereligionofpeace.com/pages/site/the-list.aspx.

3. "Report: 95 percent of Armed Conflicts Are Muslim," IsraelIslamAndEndTimes.com, December 30, 2013, http://www.israelislamandendtimes.com/report-95-violent-conflicts-around-world-muslim/.

4. "Biographical Sketch of Muhammad's Life," The Islam Project, http://www.islamproject.org/muhammad/muhammad_05_BioSketchofMuhammad.htm. See also http://www.islamreligion.com/.

5. Ibid.

6. Ahmad Shafaat, "Muhammad: The Last Prophet," Islamic Perspectives, August 2014, http://www.islamicperspectives.com/MuhammadTheLastProphet.htm.

7. "Forced Conversion," TheReligionOfPeace.com, 2014.

8. James L. Garlow, *A Christian's Response to Islam* (Colorado Springs: David C. Cook, 2005), 49–69.

9. Ibid., 49–50.

10. Drew Desilver, "World's Muslim Population More Widespread Than You Might Think," Pew Research Center, June 7, 2013, http://www.pewresearch.org/fact-tank/2013/06/07/worlds-muslim-population-more-widespread-than-you-might-think/.

11. Garlow, *A Christian's Response*, 50.

12. Ibid, 51.

13. Ibid., 74.

14. Karl Vick, "What Is the Caliphate?," *Time*, July 1, 2014, http://time.com/2942239/what-is-the-caliphate/.

15. "Sunni Rebels Declare New 'Islamic Caliphate,'" Al Jazeera, June 30, 2014, http://www.aljazeera.com/news/middleeast/2014/06/isil-declares-new-islamic-caliphate-201462917326669749.html.

16. Joseph E. B. Lumbard, "New Horizons for the Influence of American Muslim Intellectuals in the Arab World," in *Muslims in the United States: Identity, Influence, and Innovation* (Washington, DC: Woodrow Wilson International Center of Scholars, 2005), 155.

17. Institute for National Strategic Studies, *Global Strategic Assessment 2009: America's Security Role in a Changing World* (Washington, DC: U.S Government Printing Office, 2009), 124.

18. "World Watch List," OpenDoorsUSA.org, https://www.opendoorsusa.org/christian-persecution/world-watch-list/.

19. *World Report 2015: Saudi Arabia*, (Washington, DC: Human Rights Watch, 2015), https://www.hrw.org/world-report/2015/country-chapters/saudi-arabia.

20. "About the List of Attacks." "Islamic Terrorists Have Carried Out More than 28,348 Deadly Attacks since 9/11," www.thereligionofpeace.com (as of March 14, 2016, 10:30pm Pacific Time, U.S.).

CHAPTER TWENTY-EIGHT: REFUGEES

1. Emma Lazarus, "The New Colossus," Poetry Foundation, http://www.poetryfoundation.org/poem/175887.

2. David A. Graham, "Violence Has Forced 60 Million People from Their Homes," *Atlantic*, June 17, 2015, http://www.theatlantic.com/international/archive/2015/06/refugees-global-peace-index/396122.

3. Mark Bixler and Michael Martinez, "War Has Forced Half of Syrians from Their Homes, Here's Where They've Gone," CNN.com, September 11, 2015, http://www.cnn.com/2015/09/11/world/syria-refugee-crisis-when-war-displaces-half-a-country/.

4. Graham, "Violence."

5. Michael Boorstein, "The U.S. House Just Voted Unanimously That the Islamic State Commits 'Genocide,' Now What?," *Washington Post*, March 15, 2016, https://www.washingtonpost.com/news/acts-of-faith/wp/2016/03/15/the-u.s.-house-just-voted-unanimously-that-the-islamic-state-commits-genocide-now-what./

6.   John F. Kennedy, "Ich Bin Ein Berliner," June 26, 1963, available online at http://millercenter.org/president/speeches/speech-3376.

7.   Ibid.

8.   Nina Shea, "For Christians and Yazidis Fleeing Genocide, the Obama Administration Has No Room at the Inn," *National Review*, September 22, 2015, http://www.nationalreview.com/article/424401/christians-yazidis-persecuted-iraq-syria-refugees-excluded.

CHAPTER TWENTY-NINE: MEDIA

1.   "Constitution of the Commonwealth of Massachusetts," Amendments, Art. XLVIII, The Initiative, II, sec. 2, https://malegislature.gov/Laws/Constitution.

2.   Will Rogers Memorial Museums, http://www.willrogers.com/quotes.html.

3.   "Trust and Satisfaction with the National News Media," survey done by Sacred Heart University, reported in "Exhibit 2-21:Trust and Satisfaction with the National Media," Media Research Center, 2009, http://www.mrc.org/media-bias-101/exhibit-2-21-trust-and-satisfaction-national-media-2009.

4.   "Press Widely Criticized, but Trusted More Than Other Information Sources," Pew Research Center, September 22, 2011, http://www.people-press.org/2011/09/22/press-widely-criticized-but-trusted-more-than-other-institutions/.

5.   "Press Accuracy Rating Hits Two Decade Low," Pew Research Center, September 13, 2009, http://www.people-press.org/2009/09/13/press-accuracy-rating-hits-two-decade-low/.

6.   "Social Scientists Say Everyone Is Biased—and We All Have a Bias Blind Spot about It," Science20.com, June 10, 2015, http://www.science20.com/news_articles/social_scientists_say_everyone_is_biased_and_we_all_have_a_bias_blind_spot_about_it-156029?utm_source=social&utm_medium=twitter&utm_campaign=prbuexperts.

7. Lars Willnat and David H. Weaver, *The American Journalist in the Digital Age: Key Findings* (Bloomington, IN: School of Journalism, Indiana University, 2014), 9.

8. Ibid.

9. S. Robert Lichter, *The Media Elite* (Winter Park, FL: Hastings House, 1990), cited in "Exhibit 1-1: The Media Elit," Media Research Center, http://archive.mrc.org/static/biasbasics/Exhibit1-1TheMediaElite.aspx.

10. Kenneth Walsh, *Feeding the Beast* (New York: Random House, 1996), cited in "Team Clinton," Media Research Center, August 1, 1996, http://archive.mrc.org/specialreports/1996/clinton/stats.asp.

11. John Tierney, "Political Points," *New York Times*, August 1, 2004, http://www.nytimes.com/2004/08/01/us/political-points.html.

12. "Slate Votes: Obama Wins in a Rout," Slate.com, October 28, 2008, http://www.slate.com/articles/news_and_politics/politics/2008/10/slate_votes.html.

13. "Media Bias 101," Media Research Center, May 19, 2014, http://www.mrc.org/media-bias-101/media-bias-101-what-journalists-really-think-and-what-public-thinks-about-them.

CHAPTER THIRTY: NULLIFICATION AND CIVIL DISOBEDIENCE

1. "Benjamin Franklin's Great Seal Design," February 12, 1833, http://greatseal.com/committees/firstcomm/reverse.html.

2. Wayne Grudem, *Politics according to the Bible* (Grand Rapids, MI: Zondervan, 2010) 89.

3. "Alien and Sedition Acts," Library of Congress, https://www.loc.gov/rr/program/bib/ourdocs/Alien.html.

4. *The Papers of Thomas Jefferson*, vol. 30: *1 January 1798 to 31 January 1799* (Princeton University Press, 2003), 529–56.

5. "Tenth Amendment—U.S. Constitution," FindLaw.com, http://constitution.findlaw.com/amendment10.html.

6. Ibid.

7. "Nullifying the Fugitive Slave Act," CampaignForLiberty.org, http://www.campaignforliberty.org/nullifying-the-fugitive-slave-act.

8. Cited by Dr. Julian Heicklen in "Jury Nullification," June 2000, http://www.spectacle.org/0600/heicklen.html. According to numerous sources, Chase made this quote in 1796.

9. Harlan Stone, "The Common Law in the United States," *Harvard Legal Review* 4, no. 10 (1936).

10. Martin Luther King Jr., "Letter from a Birmingham Jail," April 16, 1963, https://kinginstitute.stanford.edu/king-papers/documents/letter-birmingham-jail.

11. Brian Edwards, "Tyndale's Betrayal and Death," *Christianity Today*, 1987, http://www.christianitytoday.com/history/issues/issue-16/tyndales-betrayal-and-death.html.

12. Ibid.

13. Ibid.

14. "Testimonials to Thomas More's Greatness: II," The Center for Thomas More Studies, http://www.thomasmorestudies.org/rep_lawyer.html.

15. "Pledge in Solidarity to Defend Marriage," DefendMarriage.org, http://defendmarriage.org/pledge-in-solidarity-to-defend-marriage.

16. "Manhattan Declaration: A Call of Christian Conscience," released November 20, 2009, http://manhattandeclaration.org/#2.

CHAPTER THIRTY-ONE: A CALL TO ACTION AND THE REASON FOR HOPE

1. "Marco: All the Answers Are in the Bible," audio of Marco Rubio, YouTube video uploaded by "Larry Simmons," February 22, 2016, https://www.youtube.com/watch?v=hrcwc0XkoOo.

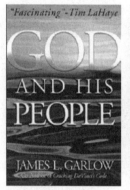

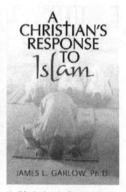
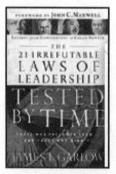

Heaven and the Afterlife
(2009, 200 pgs.)

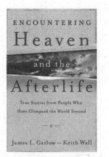

Encountering Heaven and the Afterlife
(2010, 284 pgs.)

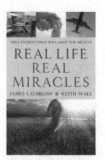

Real Life Real Miracles
(2012, 272 pgs.)

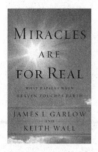

Miracles are for Real
(2011, 272 pgs.)

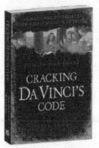

Cracking Da Vinci's Code
(2004, 248 pgs.)

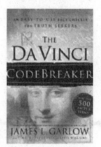

Da Vinci's Codebreaker
(2006, 203 pgs.)

The Secret Revealed
(2007, 295 pgs.)

The Blood Covenant
(2013, 192 pgs.)